Aristotle's Poetics

ARISTOTLE'S POETICS

*Translated with Commentaries
and Glossary by*
**HIPPOCRATES G. APOSTLE
ELIZABETH A. DOBBS
MORRIS A. PARSLOW**

THE PERIPATETIC PRESS
Grinnell, Iowa

Copyright © 1990 by the Peripatetic Press
pa. ISBN 0-911589-09-0
Library of Congress catalog card number: 89-64029
Manufactured in the United States of America

To Sheldon P. Zitner

Table of Contents

FOREWORD

This fresh translation of Aristotle's *Poetics* is an attempt to place before a wide public an accurate rendering into current English of the most influential work of literary criticism in Western culture. One may dispute the correctness of Alfred North Whitehead's saying that all philosophy is a set of footnotes to Plato, but there is no doubt that subsequent literary criticism, at least in Europe and the Americas, follows in the paths first opened up by Aristotle.

The *Poetics* has set the agenda for the discussion not only of tragic drama, but of literature as a whole. The *Poetics* offers, among other contributions to literary criticism, a complex and subtle definition of tragedy, an acute model for the analysis of tragic plot, an extended contrast between dramatic and narrative form, and suggestive treatments of character, spectacle, and language. In addition to this, Aristotle offers conceptions of the aims of art and its psychological basis and conceptual tools for determining its kinds and modes. He also suggests some of the pitfalls encountered in the typical procedures of literary criticism.

Particularly from the Renaissance on, the *Poetics* has been the foundation of both literary theory and "practical" criticism, and it has been translated and re–translated, interpreted, applied, and cited in polemics as a final authority. Indeed, the seventeenth–century English satiric poet, Samuel Butler, complained that

> "No pudding [clown] will be suffered to be witty
> Unless it be to terrify or pity,"

and Horace Walpole, equally aware of his contemporaries' obsession with the *Poetics*, amused himself with giving thanks that Aristotle had come after rather than before Homer, thus sparing the epic poet the labor of strict conformity to the ultimate critic. The ossification of ideas often attributed to Aristotle during the Enlightenment was only

one kind of distortion to which the *Poetics* has been subject. Throughout the history of its transmission, translation, and interpretation, the
understanding of the *Poetics* has been subject to errors due to faulty
texts or uninformed translation, or to distortions arising from interpretations peculiar to the critic or to the attitudes and concerns of a
particular period or school of thought. It should come as no surprise
that some Victorian and early twentieth–century translators and critics thought that Aristotle's term "*hamartia*" (best understood as "mistake" or "error") was properly rendered by a phrase such as "tragic
flaw," with its overtones of moral defect and culpability. Such a rendering answered to the moralizing tendencies of those critics, although it clearly led to the contradiction of Aristotle's thought
elsewhere in the *Poetics*. Aristotle condemns as weak and untragic the
"double ending" in which the bad are punished and the good re-
warded or left unharmed. But to think of errors in judgment made by
the protagonists of tragedy as guilty errors is to see all tragedies as
tending to punitive outcomes, hardly Aristotle's intention.

Similarly, the so–called "Revolution of the Word" associated with
modern poets like T.S. Eliot and with the American "New Critics"
(Cleanth Brooks, Robert Penn Warren, *et al.*) has led some to question
the usefulness of the *Poetics* because of its supposed neglect of *lexis*, a
concern with language and particularly diction and syntax. Admit-
tedly, it is difficult to apply to modern English the kinds of analysis
Aristotle proposes as relevant to classical Greek. But properly understood, the principles he states *are* applicable. In any case, the isolation by some recent critics of the study of diction and syntax from
their contexts (i.e. from plot and character) neglects the common experience of how ambiguous and mercurial language can be apart from
such contexts and ignores the consequence that only within such
contexts do the meanings and emotional tones of language become
clear. These instances are offered not only as evidence that the *Poetics*
can be and has been misinterpreted in the course of time. They are offered as evidence also of the continuing relevance of Aristotle's work
to the changing issues in literary criticism.

Because of the nature of the text and the history of its transmission,
some scholars have thought that the *Poetics* suffers from vital omis-
sions or arbitrary emphases in the materials it presents. No doubt the
text of the *Poetics* as we have it would differ from the text Aristotle
might give us if he were alive today. But the textual difficulties have

been exaggerated and, more importantly, the *Poetics* does not exist in isolation. It is one of many works by Aristotle: some of its concerns are taken up in his *Rhetoric* and *Ethics*; its terminology is wholly consistent with his usage elsewhere; its methods of analysis and reasoning are elaborated in his other philosophic works.

The present translation draws on the translator's previous work with other important Aristotelian texts, and so avoids the errors of earlier translators, who have sometimes failed to appreciate how apparent difficulties and gaps in meaning in the *Poetics* can be clarified by an appreciation of Aristotle's modes of reasoning and expression elsewhere. This translation approaches the *Poetics* in the belief that it is not the work of student note–takers (clearly an impossibility in view of the circumstances of its delivery and the nature of the text itself) and that it is not grossly incomplete or unintelligible. Yet translation is a human effort, and in the nature of things no human effort achieves perfection. Moreover, both literary criticism and the works it treats are far more problematic than, say, mathematics or its subject–matter; hence the particular difficulties that await both the translator and the interpreter of the *Poetics*. But if ideal translation cannot be attained, it can at least be approached. That is the aim of this translation of the *Poetics*. Its novelty as well as its strength lies in its search, through the contemporary idiom, for language that reflects the consistency and clarity of Aristotle's thought not only in the *Poetics* but throughout his works.

The translation of the *Poetics* is the latest in Professor Apostle's ongoing project of re–presenting the major works of Aristotle to English–speaking readers. In its striving for accuracy, clarity and universality—that is, its attempt to employ terminology consistent with Aristotelian usage throughout the canon—the project is reminiscent of the great undertakings of Renaissance humanism or Victorian classical scholarship. Professor Apostle has persevered in his labors despite obstacles that go beyond their inherent difficulties, and his efforts have met with the appreciation and gratitude of numerous scholars in various fields of philosophy, political science and the history of science. With this edition of the *Poetics*, a more general audience will now be indebted to his efforts.

Sheldon P. Zitner
Trinity College, Toronto

PREFACE

The *Poetics* is perhaps the most difficult of Aristotle's works to translate accurately and to make reliable comments on. This becomes evident if the difficulties faced by the translator are pointed out.

We have shown in the "Theory of Art", Part V, of this work that, according to Aristotle, the *Poetics* is a scientific work. Now, translation is a relation like teaching, whose three essential elements are the teacher, the nature of the subject taught, and the student. Similarly, the elements of a translation are (1) the author of the work to be translated, (2) the nature of the work to be translated, and (3) the translator. The principles of translating the *Poetics*, then, would be those of translating a scientific work; and since the proper aim of a science as a science is truth, the translator must see to it that the accuracy of the thought in the *Poetics* and the truth of the comments on that thought are preserved in the translation, all other elements being of little importance in the translation as such. Consequently, flowery and emotional language, foreign terms, and other kinds of embellishments in the translation of this work should be avoided or kept to a minimum, for at best they contribute nothing and at worst they distort the accuracy of the original thought and the truth of the comments on that thought. In short, since the *Poetics* was written as a science and not as a work of art, one should translate it as a science and not as if it were a work of art.

But sciences differ by their nature with respect to their accuracy and in three main ways: they are less accurate (a) quantitatively, if their principles are more numerous; (b) qualitatively, if their subjects admit of higher degree of variation or are less definite or less clearly understood; and (c) logically, if more theorems in them are left undemonstrated; for, by definition, sciences require demonstrations of their theorems (87a31–37). Consequently, translations of scientific works tend to vary in accuracy with respect to (a) or (b) or (c).

First, let us turn to (1) the author, i.e., to Aristotle as the author of the *Poetics* and of the rest of his scientific works. In spite of contrary claims, those who have adequate knowledge of ancient Greek and both extensive and intensive understanding of at least the major works attributed to him would hardly find statements in them which lead to contradiction or, in many cases, what some might consider to be subject to interpretation. The works considered to represent Aristotle's thought are highly consistent logically and methodologically and terminologically; the terms in them are adequately defined in the various works where they belong; and any statements in them which are no longer held as being true in view of new information are either principles laid down by him or conclusions deducible from premises, some of which are based on those principles, in which case the errors committed are not due to inconsistency. Variants in the manuscripts due to text corruption, miscopying, attempts to correct other manuscripts, or other such reasons do not alter the fact that what we possess are, as a whole, the writings of Aristotle. The *Athenian Constitution* appears to be an exception, not by departing from Aristotle's thought, but by being written in a style or manner which Aristotle would not use; perhaps it was one of the many constitutions written by assistants and used by Aristotle in writing his *Politics*. Further, the opinion which still lingers to some extent today—that some or all of the works which have come down to us are not Aristotle's own writings but notes taken by his students—is incredible for three good reasons: (a) it cannot be supported by an analysis and organization of the various works and by comparison with what one would expect from notes taken by students at a time when note–taking was slower than it is nowadays; (b) if the notes were taken exactly as they were spoken by their master, they would still represent Aristotle's exact thought and should not be called "notes taken by students"; and (c) it is ridiculous to think that more care was taken by the directors of the Peripatetic School to preserve for posterity notes by students than to preserve Aristotle's own writings. In short, the scientific manner in which Aristotle's works are written is fairly accurate, and errors appearing in translations or in comments on the *Poetics* in particular should hardly be regarded as due to Aristotle's presentation of this work.

Turning to (2), the nature of the work to be translated, we find that it is suggested by the definition of tragedy, whose main part, the plot, is concerned with human *actions*; and these, being numerous in kind and involving such elements as feelings, virtues, justice, and the like, admit variations of degree. Consequently, other things being equal, translations of the *Poetics* cannot be expected to possess the high accuracy one finds in translations of mathematical or logical works.

Most of the errors in a translation of and comments on the *Poetics* are due to (3), the translator, and it is reasonable to expect this from the nature of this work. If the translator is a mathematician and the work to be translated is mathematical, even an ancient work such as *Euclid's Elements*, usually the translation will be free from error, and so will the comments on that work; for the terms in that science are few, well–defined, and familiar to mathematicians, and comments on that work will usually be agreed upon. But if the translator is in the field of literature and is not a scientist, which is usually the case, and the work to be translated is the *Poetics*, the difficulties faced are enormous, unless the translator is a genius by nature. First, not being a scientist, the translator will hardly be adequately familiar with scientific methodology, and the comments on the method used in that work are likely to be less true or accurate than the corresponding comments of the above–mentioned mathematician on a mathematical work. Second, some of the terms in the *Poetics* belong to Aristotle's *Categories, Metaphysics, Physics, Ethics, Posterior Analytics* and to other of the major works, and scientific knowledge of those terms is necessary if errors in translating them are to be avoided. Third, and above all, those terms are elements in statements, and as such they are not scientifically investigated but only applied in the statements of the *Poetics*; but if they are to be understood scientifically in the *Poetics*—and they must be so understood—they should be studied scientifically in those works where they belong. Such understanding would entail many years of intensive and extensive study of the major works of Aristotle, at least to the extent needed for the understanding of the *Poetics*, for knowledge of their definitions alone is not adequate. Can a translator whose field is literature, already flooded with work in his own field, afford such lengthy study? Conversely, one who has done such a study but is in a field other than literature would have difficulties similar or analogous to those of a person in the field of literature in translating the *Poetics*; for understanding in the field of literature would require, among other things, powers of intuition and perception which, as powers, must be developed as well as inherited.

Clearly, then, extensive and intensive knowledge of Aristotle's major works to the extent needed in understanding the *Poetics* would substantially eliminate errors in translating accurately and commenting reliably on that work. Such vast knowledge can hardly be possessed by one thinker; but it could exist in a number of thinkers who together possess all the parts of such knowledge and who work as a unit. It is in view of the difficulties indicated that we have sought the required aid from many such thinkers so as to minimize errors to the best of our ability.

Since readability and accuracy of scientific thought in a translation of the *Poetics* are highly desirable, the English terms into which the Greek terms are translated should be familiar, clear, definite in meaning, adequate, and consistent. The terms should be familiar, for unfamiliar terms require unnecessary effort of the mind without contributing anything; they should be clear, for lack of clarity tends to cloud thought or the intellect; they should be definite in meaning, and this is facilitated by definitions or explanations or examples or in some other ways; they should be adequate, for, to take an example, distinctions may be lost if terms in the original differing in meaning are identified as synonyms; and they should be consistent, for otherwise they may lead to contradictions or fail to convey the original thought. The use of English synonyms for the sake of variety or of such devices as foreign terms and poetic expressions should be avoided or kept to a minimum, for they have no place in scientific thought. For the sake of uniformity and convenience, the English terms common to the *Poetics* and the other translations published by the Peripatetic Press have, in general, the same meanings.

An important principle of translating the *Poetics* into English is the following: "An English term into which a Greek term is translated must have the same meaning as the corresponding Greek term; but if no such English term exists, the English term chosen for the Greek term should be such that its meaning is closest to the meaning of the Greek term." So if, in the absence of an English term, the meaning of the English term chosen is closest to that of the Greek term, the translator should state the reason for his choice in order to prevent the reader from being misled in thought; otherwise unfair criticism would follow. An obvious example which led to unfair criticism is the choice of the term "poem" for the Greek term transliterated as "*poiema*." The usual objection raised by some is that Aristotle had a narrow conception of a poem. But if the translator states that there is no English term having the meaning of "*poiema*" and that the term "poem" has been chosen for lack of a better term, specifying at the same time what that meaning of "poem" will be in the translation, the reader will have no good reason to raise the objection mentioned. Many such objections have been raised against Aristotle's use of terms and statements in the *Poetics* and in his other works.

One way of facilitating the reader's getting the thought of the *Poetics* accurately is to include a glossary of terms, especially if the reader's first contact with the works of Aristotle is the *Poetics*; another is to make commentaries; a third is to give references to his other works; a fourth is to introduce typographical conventions, for confusion is often possible without them, and to these we now turn.

Since a term, whether vocal or graphic, differs from what it signifies, we will enclose it with quotation marks when we refer to it. For example, the word "apple" so enclosed is a noun and not a fruit; and the same may be said of the expression "four is a square integer," which is a statement and not a fact, although it signifies a fact. Similar remarks shall apply to concepts and *thoughts*, for they are analogous to terms and expressions, respectively, and differ from what they stand for. As a thought, for example, "five" is a concept and not a number, and the *thought* "Plato was a philosopher" is true, for it is a proposition existing primarily in the mind, and truth exists primarily in the mind. The quotation marks may be left out if the subordinating conjunction "that" is used before a statement or a *thought*. We may say, for example, the *thought* that the earth is flat is false instead of the *thought* "the earth is flat" is false. For convenience, Greek words or expressions will not be enclosed in quotation marks. We will say, for example, that ποσόν is a Greek word which will be translated as "quantity."

Terms or expressions in italics will be used in four different ways: (1) for the sake of emphasis; (2) if a Greek word is transliterated into English, the English word will be printed in italics (for example, the word ποίημα is transliterated as "*Poiema*"); (3) to avoid introducing a new name, in some cases Aristotle uses the same name sometimes as a genus but at other times as a species, and to make the distinction, we will translate that name into English in roman letters when used as a genus but in italics when used as a species. For example, the word αὐτόματον is translated as "chance" when used as a genus, but as "*chance*" when used as a species (see Glossary); (4) In English, too, we will avoid introducing a new name in a few cases but use the same name in roman letters as a genus but in italics as a species, as in the names "thought" and "*thought.*"

Words or expressions within brackets are not translations from the Greek but are added for the sake of the reader. In the first paragraph of the translation of the *Poetics,* for example, we added the phrase "of each species should have" within brackets to clarify Aristotle's meaning.

In English dictionaries, two of the meanings of the word "man" are (a) a male or female human being and (b) a male human being. In Greek, the corresponding words are transliterated into English as (a) "*anthropos*" and (b) "*aner,*" respectively, and the word for a woman is transliterated as "*gyne.*" We will use "man" for a male or female human being, "*man*" for a male human being and "woman" for a female human being. Linguistically, the word "*anthropos*" is masculine, and the corresponding Greek pronouns referring to it are also masculine. In view of this, we will use "he," "his," and "him" instead of "he or she," "his or her," and "him or her," respectively, when referring to both sexes or when referring to the masculine sex, and the usual "she" or "her" when referring to a woman. In this manner, the distinctions in Greek will be retained in English. This change, however, will be limited to the translation and partly to the Commentaries and Theory of Art in order to avoid distortion of Aristotle's thought.

In the margins of the translation we have inserted the pages and lines according to the Bekker text, which is standard. The various works of Aristotle we possess and the corresponding Bekker pages containing each of them are listed at the beginning of the Commentaries. Since there are many variants in the different manuscripts that have come down to us, our policy in translating the *Poetics* has been (a) to choose those variants which in our opinion agree or are consistent with Aristotle's *thought,* and if, in some cases, we disagree with all the variants of an expression, (b) to introduce our own variant and add a commentary giving the reason for our disagreement.

We do not know whether Aristotle wrote a work on art; but, from the various remarks he made about art, it is possible to present a fairly accurate account of his position on that subject. We have undertaken to present such a theory by including, with some references, "Aristotle's Theory of Art" in this work. One should regard this part, then, as being written by Aristotelians, i.e., by those who present Aristotle's thought to the extent they understand it.

Many have contributed in making this work possible. We are grateful to Professors James A. Arieti, Laurence B. Berns, Michael W. Cavanagh, Peter J. Connelly, James D. Kissane, Gerald V. Lalonde, Myron M. Liberman, Peter L. DeLuca III, Donald G. Marshall, Johann M. Moser, Sheldon P. Zitner, the Rev. Ronald K. Tacelli, and to the late John M. Crossett who aided us extensively in the early stages of the translation of the *Poetics*.

Grinnell College
H.G.A.
E.A.D.
M.A.P.

SUMMARY OF THE POETICS

1. Poetics is neither a theoretical nor a practical but a productive science, and its subject is the art of making poems in general. There are many species of the poetic art and many productive sciences corresponding to those species. Two species of the poetic art are the art of tragedy and the art of comedy.

The proximate genus of poems in general is "imitation with a plot." Poems differ from each other (a) by using different means or materials in their composition, (b) by imitating different objects, and (c) by imitating their objects in a different manner.

2. The objects imitated by poems are *actions* of men; and just as men are virtuous or vicious or partake of both virtue and vice, so do their *actions*.

3. A poem may be either (1) narrated by one man, whether by the poet or by one who represents the poet, or (2) dramatized by performers who represent the characters or agents in the poem. If narrated, it may be done by the narrator either (1a) in his own person or (1b) dramatically, i.e., by changing and so representing now one agent and now another.

4. The origin and development of the art of poetry is due to two causes, the moving and the final: (1) man by his nature is born with the potentiality to imitate; and (2) he enjoys imitative works of art or producing such works. In fact, man is the most imitative of all animals. Thus, man as an artist is the mover who imitates by producing tragedies, and man's enjoyment by seeing tragedies performed (and perhaps by producing tragedies) is the final cause.

5. One species of the art of poetry is the art of comedy. Some remarks about its history. Comedy differs from tragedy by imitating a different kind of object; epic differs from tragedy in the manner in which it is presented.

6. The definition of tragedy is derived from the foregoing discus-

sions, and the qualitative parts—plot, character, thought, diction, song, and spectacle—are identified.

7. The plot must be a whole and complete and have a proper magnitude so that it can be easily perceived and remembered.

8. The unity of the plot must depend on the unity of the *action* imitated, not on the unity of one man's history or of one period, which is accidental to one *action*.

9. The unity of the *action* in a poem is due to the fact that the events in the plot from the beginning until the end follow each other causally, that is, of necessity or with probability. Historical events, on the other hand, are about particulars in time which as such do not all follow causally but most do so accidentally. Since philosophy is concerned with the causes of things and not with accidents, it would follow that poetry is more philosophical than history.

10. A simple plot in tragedy is one in which a change occurs from good fortune to misfortune without reversal or recognition; a complex plot is one in which such change occurs with reversal or recognition or both.

11. Reversal and recognition are defined and exemplified, and the best kinds are characterized.

12. The quantitative parts of tragedy are prologue, episode, exode, and choral song, the two kinds of song being parode and stasimon. Some tragedies have additional parts: songs from the stage and *commi* (i.e., lamentations).

13. The finest kind of tragedy is one in which (a) the plot is complex as defined but also single in its outcome, i.e., without also changing from misfortune to good fortune, (b) the protagonist is neither ideally virtuous nor wicked or utterly base but possesses virtue which is average or better than average, (c) the protagonist is a man of reputation and good fortune, and (d) the change to misfortune occurs because of some grave *action* performed not from wickedness or some other vice but because of an error from ignorance or bad judgment or some other such cause.

14. The best kind of plot whose tragic pleasure is most appropriate, is one in which (a) fearful and pitiful *actions* arise not from forced or artificial devices, such as *deus ex machina*, or spectacle or accidents in general, but from *actions* which follow naturally (i.e., by necessity or with probability) from the events in the plot, and (b) the protagonist

recognizes the victim just before he is about to perform the grave *action* and then does not *act*.

15. The character (i.e., the ethical quality) of an agent in the plot should (a) be cogent, i.e., be brought out clearly through his spoken words and *actions*, (b) fit the role played by the agent, (c) be similar to those in real life, and (d) be consistent or consistently inconsistent. Similarly, the events should be portrayed realistically according to necessity or probability and conform to the principles of the poetic plot.

16. Recognitions through signs and tokens and the like, devised by the poet, are rather inartistic; devices from memory or inference are better; but the best kind of recognitions should be consequences of the events themselves and brought out as such in the performance.

17. Suggestions are made to the poet in constructing a tragic plot and working out the diction. The poet should lay out a sketch of the plot, visualize and even act out whenever possible the events in it, and then make up the episodes and fill in the details.

18. Complication and resolution are defined. The poet should handle well both of these and do likewise with all the parts of tragedy or most of them and the most important. Four kinds of tragedy are listed: the complex, that of suffering, that of character; but the fourth is not specified for some reason. Tragedies are said to be the same if their plots are of the same kind. The poet should not make a tragedy out of an epic structure. The chorus should function as one of the performers.

19. *Thought* is the proper subject of the science of rhetoric and is discussed in the *Rhetoric*. The aim of *thought* is (a) arguing for or against a position, (b) rendering the emotions, and (c) maximizing or minimizing the importance or unimportance of what is to be said. Diction is the subject of the science of delivery or of a higher science; although it does not come under poetics, it should be appropriately applied to the making of poems.

20. The parts of spoken language, starting from the most elementary, are letters, syllables, connectives, joints, nouns, verbs, inflections, and speech. Their definitions are given.

21. The kinds of names with respect to their effective value in poetry are defined and discussed, especially metaphors and analogies.

22. Lucidity and dignity in diction are achieved by the use of an appropriate combination of standard and strange (i.e., non–standard) names. Metaphors are the most important of strange names in poems, and the ability to produce them is a sign of a gifted poet.

23, 24. Epic poetry is like tragedy by having the same kind of aim; it differs from tragedy by (a) being narrative and longer, (b) imitating many or different events simultaneously, (c) using the heroic meter (i.e., the hexameter), which is the most suitable to it, (d) admitting most readily foreign names and metaphors, (e) being at best when narrated dramatically, and (f) achieving special effects of wonder by admitting falsehoods and impossibilities and absurdities which transcend reason.

25. A list of the number and nature of critical problems or objections which might arise is given, and the solutions or answers to them are stated by being referred to the various principles of the poetic science.

26. Tragedy is superior to epic because: (1) it adds to their common qualitative parts the enhancements of song and spectacle; (2) it produces more vivid effects, even when it is just read; and (3) it achieves its poetic aim in a more unified and shorter time.

POETICS[1]

1

Concerning the art of poetry, both itself and its species,[2] let us 1447a speak about (a) the effect which each has,[3] (b) how plots should be constructed if the making of poems is to be done well,[4] (c) how many 10 and what kinds of parts[5] a poem [of each species should have], and similarly (d) about any other things which belong to this *inquiry*; and let us begin first with the things which are first according to nature.[6]

Productions of epic and of tragedy and, moreover, of comedy and dithyrambs and of most works for the flute and the lyre all[7] turn out to 15 be, each of them taken as a whole, [poetic] imitations.[8] These [imitations] differ from one another in three respects, for they imitate either (a) by different means[9] or (b) different objects[10] or (c) in a different and not in the same manner.[11]

Now just as some imitate many things by making likenesses of them with colors and figures,[12] either by art or by habit,[13] while others do 20 so by their nature,[14] so, too, each of the above–mentioned [poetic] arts produces its imitation in rhythm or language or harmony,[15] using these [means] either separately or in combination. For example, arts which use only harmony and rhythm are those of the flute and the lyre and any others which might happen to have a similar power, e.g., 25 the art of the Panpipe; an art which may use rhythm without harmony, on the other hand, is that of the dancers, for these artists, too, imitate character and feelings and *actions* by means of rhythmical gestures.[16]

The art that uses only language, whether in prose or in verse (and if 1447b in verse, [by] combining different meters with one another or using only one kind of meter), turns out to be nameless up to now; for we have no common name for the mimes of Sophron and Xenarchus and 10 for the Socratic dialogues,[17] nor for any imitation by means of trimeters or elegiacs or some other such meter that one might use. Men, however, adding the word "making"[18] to the meter employed, use the terms "elegiac–makers" and "epic–makers" and so call such writers "poets," doing so not with respect to their imitation of objects but with respect to the name common to the meter.[19] For even if what 15 is produced is a work on medicine or physics written in meters, they are accustomed to speak of it in this way. But there is nothing common

to Homer and Empedocles except the meter; and so the one should
justly be called "a poet" whereas the other should be called "a natural
20   philosopher" rather than "a poet."[20] In like manner, if one were to
produce an imitation by combining all the meters (as Chaeremon did
in his *Centaur*, a rhapsody combined from all the meters), he should
be called "a poet" [in virtue of his imitation alone].[21]

Let the distinctions about these matters, then, be made in this way.
There are, however, some [poets] who use all the three means men-
25   tioned above, that is, rhythm and song and meter, as indeed we find in
the making of (a) dithyrambs and nomes, and of (b) tragedies and
comedies; but they differ in this respect: the former use all the means
simultaneously, the latter use them in turn.[22]

Among the arts, then, I say these are the different means by which
those artists produce their imitation.

2

1448*a*   Since those[1] who engage in [poetic] imitation imitate [men] in *action*, who must therefore be either virtuous or vicious (for character[2]
is almost always attributed to these two kinds of men alone, inasmuch
as all men differ with respect to character in virtue and vice and so are
5   either better than average or worse than average or about average),
just as painters do (for Polygnotus made likenesses of better men,
Pauson of worse men, and Dionysius of men about average), it is clear
that each of the [three kinds of] imitations mentioned will also differ
from the other [kinds] by imitating in the same way men of one kind
[of character] only.[3] These dissimilarities may occur even in dancing
10   and flute–playing and lyre–playing, and the same may be said also of
prose and verse without harmony.[4] Thus Homer imitates better men,
Cleophon imitates average men, but Hegemon of Thasos, the first to
write parodies, imitates worse men, and so does Nicochares, the au-
15   thor of the *Deiliad*.[5] And this applies similarly to dithyrambs and to
nomes. One might imitate men as[6] ..., and as Timotheus and
Philoxenus did in their *Cyclopes*. Likewise, tragedy and comedy are
distinguished by the same kinds of differences; for comedy sets out to
imitate men who are worse than average, and tragedy men who are
better than average.

3

Imitations may differ in yet a third way: the manner in which one might imitate the objects [in each art]. For it is possible to imitate the   20 same objects with the same means: (1) by narration, either (a) when the narrator[1] speaks in his own person at one time but assumes the role of someone else at another time, as Homer does, or (b) when the narrator speaks in his own person without changing, or (2) when the performers dramatize in the poem all the agents who are engaged in *action* or in other kinds of activity.[2]

As we said at the beginning, then, the differences in imitation are   25 three: the *means*, the *objects*, and the *manner*.[3] So, in one respect, Sophocles would be the same kind of imitator as Homer, for both produce imitations of virtuous men;[4] in another respect, he would be the same in kind as Aristophanes, for both produce imitations of agents in *action* portrayed dramatically.[5] It is in view of this fact that some say that these [i.e., tragedy and comedy] are also called "dramas" [= "*dramata*"] inasmuch as performers in them dramatize [= *drondas*] agents in the poems.[6] For this reason, the Dorians[7] claim the discov-   30 ery of both tragedy and comedy. For (1) the Megarians[8] claim comedy: (a) those here in the mainland of Greece on the grounds that it arose in the time of their popular rule and (b) those from Sicily, for the poet Epicharmus[9] came from there and lived much earlier than Chionides and Magnes;[10] and (2) some of the Peloponnesians claim   35 tragedy by pointing to the names "drama" and "comedy" as a sign of their claim. For the Dorians say that they call the suburbs "*comae*," whereas the Athenians call them "*demes*," and from this fact the Dorians argue that the word "*comodoi*" (= "comedians") came not from the verb "*comazein*" (= "to revel") but from the wandering of the comedians among the *comae*, since they were held in low esteem and were driven out of the city. The Dorians say also that for the word   1448*b* "*poein*" (= "doing") they use the word "*dran*," whereas the Athenians use the word "*prattein*" (= "acting").[11]

Concerning imitations with respect to the number and nature of their differences, then, let the above suffice.

4

It is reasonable to think that the art of poetry in general was brought into being by two kinds of causes, both of them natural;[1] for (1) imitat-   5

ing is innate in men from childhood,[2] and in this respect men differ
from the other animals by being the most imitative of animals and
learning first by imitating,[3] and (2) all men enjoy works of imitation.[4]

10 A sign of the second cause is what happens when we observe works [of
art]; for, although we are pained while observing certain objects, we
nevertheless enjoy beholding their likenesses if these have been care-
fully worked out with special accuracy, e.g., likenesses of the forms of
the lowest animals and of corpses. And the *reason* for this enjoyment
is that learning is pleasant—indeed most pleasant— not only for philosophers, but similarly for other men also, although the latter par-

15 take of such pleasure only to some extent. That is why men enjoy
observing likenesses: as they behold them, they learn and infer what
each likeness portrays, e.g., that this is a likeness of that [man]; and if
one happens not to have observed earlier the object imitated, pleasure will still come, not because the work is an imitation, but because
of the workmanship or the coloring or some other such *reason*.[5]

20 Since imitating and also using harmony and rhythm come to us according to our nature (for it is evident that meters are parts of
rhythm), those who at first had the greatest gifts for these, by gradually improving on them, gave birth to the making of poetry out of
improvisations.[6] But this activity went forward in two directions in ac-

25 cordance with the character [of each imitator]; for the more dignified
poets were imitating noble *actions* or the *actions* of noble men,[7]
whereas the less worthy poets were imitating the *actions* of inferior
men,[8] first making invectives just as the others were making hymns
and encomia. Now of the poets before Homer we can cite no poems of
this [lampooning] sort, though it is likely that there were many such

30 poets; but starting from Homer we can give examples, e.g., his
Margites and other such poems, in which the fitting meter, the iambic, came into use; and it was for this reason that these poems are now
called "iambics,"[9] since in this meter the poets lampooned one another. Thus some of the ancient poets became makers of heroic
poems, others of iambics, i.e., of lampooning poems.

35 Now just as Homer as a poet excelled in serious subjects (for he was
unique not only in making his imitations well, but in making them dramatic also), so, too, he was the first to indicate by example the forms
of comedy, dramatizing[10] not invective but the ludicrous. There is in-

1449a deed an analogy: as the *Iliad* and the *Odyssey* are to tragedies, so the
Margites is to comedies.[11] Once tragedy and comedy appeared on the

scene, of those who pursued each of these two species of poetry in accordance with their special nature, some became comic instead of
iambic poets, others became tragedians[12] instead of epic poets, because the forms of comedy and tragedy were grander and more es-
teemed than those of iambic and epic, respectively.

To examine whether or not tragedy is at present adequate in its
kinds,[13] judged both with respect to its nature as such and in relation
to the theater, is another matter.[14] In any case, tragedy and comedy
started from improvisations, tragedy from those who introduced the
dithyramb, comedy from those who introduced the phallic performances which still, even now, remain the custom in many states. Then
[tragedy] grew gradually as the poets made advancements by adding
what appeared to be appropriate to it, and, having undergone many
changes, it ceased to change when it attained its nature. Aeschylus
was the first to raise the number of performers from one to two, to
lessen the role of the chorus, and to give speech the leading role;
Sophocles added a third performer and scenery. Furthermore, after a
period of short plots and ludicrous diction, which were characteristic
of early tragedy because of its change from satyric form, the size of
tragic plots after a long time achieved dignity, and the meter likewise
changed from [trochaic] tetrameter to iambic [trimeter]; for at first
[tragic] poets used the [trochaic] tetrameter because poetry then was
satyric and more associated with dance, but when diction [like that of
ordinary speech] came in, nature herself found the appropriate
meter, for the iambic meter is the most characteristic of conversation.
A sign of this is the fact that we use mostly iambs in our conversation
with one another, but we seldom speak in hexameters, and when we
do, we depart from the spoken intonation which characterizes [ordi-
nary] speech. Furthermore, as to how the number of episodes has
changed and how each of the other [parts of the tragedy] are said to
have been enhanced, let it be enough for us to have mentioned them,
for it would perhaps be a big task to go through them individually.

5

Comedy, as we have said,[1] is an imitation of men worse than average, not with respect to every kind of vice but with respect to the ludicrous part of the ugly;[2] for the ludicrous part is a kind of error or
ugliness[3] that is neither distressing nor destructive, such as, to take an

*- comedy ugly
because things are
distorted*

obvious example, the comic mask, which is in some sense ugly and distorted but causes no distress.

Now the changes in tragedy and those who made them have not gone unnoticed. Comedy, on the other hand, has gone unnoticed from the beginning because it was not taken seriously; for the archon authorized a chorus of comic performers at quite a late date, but until then there were only volunteers. It was when comedy had already taken on certain forms that those who were called "comic poets" were [first] recorded. But we do not know who it was who provided it with masks or prologues or a number of performers or other such things. Plots were first produced by Epicharmus and Phormis, who came [to Athens] from Sicily, while of the comic poets of Athens, Crates was the first to drop the lampooning kind of comedy and use language and plots of a universal nature.[4]

Epic poetry and tragedy are alike insofar as both imitate serious [matters] in grand meter and language; but (a) epic poetry differs from tragedy in using one [kind of] meter[5] and in being narrative in manner. Furthermore, it differs in length; for tragedy attempts as far as possible to be complete within one revolution of the sun,[6] or to vary from this time period only by a little; but epic poetry has no definite limits in time, and in this respect it differs from tragedy, although at first the poets set no definite limits of time in tragedies as well as in epics. As for the parts,[7] some are the same for both, whereas others are proper to tragedy. In view of this, whoever understands good and bad tragedy also understands good and bad epic poetry, for the parts of epic poetry are present in tragedy, but not all the parts of tragedy are present in epic poetry.

6

Concerning imitative poetry in hexameters[1] and comedy we shall speak later. Let us now speak of tragedy, taking out from what has been said so far about it those parts which give rise to the definition of its essence.

Tragedy, then, is (1) an imitation of an *action* which is serious and complete and has a [proper] magnitude, (2) [expressed] in speech with forms of enhancements appropriate to each of its parts and used separately, (3) [presented] by performers in a dramatic and not a narrative manner, and (4) ending through pity and fear in a catharsis of such emotions.[2]

By "speech with forms of enhancements" I mean speech which has   30
rhythm or intonation or song;[3] by "appropriate to each of its parts" I
mean that the poet achieves some of his ends through meter alone
and others through song [...].   Parts of tragic play

Since it is by *action* that [performers] produce their imitation, first
the enhancement by spectacle would necessarily be a part of tragedy,
and then the use of song and diction; for it is by means of these that
[tragic performers] produce their imitation. By "diction" here I mean,
[for example], the combination of the parts; by "use of song" I mean,   35
that whose effect is evident to everybody.

Since imitation [in tragedy] is of an *action*,[4] and since *actions* are
willed by men, who must have certain qualities, namely, character
and *thought* (for it is because of these that *actions*, too, are said to be   1450a
of a certain kind),[5] there are by nature two causes of *actions*, namely,
thought and character; and it is in virtue of these that all men succeed
or fail.[6] Now the imitation of the *action* is the plot, for by "plot" here I
mean the combination of the events; by "character" I mean that in vir-   5
tue of which we say that men in *action* are of a certain quality; and by
"*thought*" I mean that quality by means of which men say when they
argue for or against something or express a *judgment*.[7]

Every tragedy, then, must use six parts in virtue of which it is a tragedy of a certain quality. These are plot, character, diction, *thought*,   10
spectacle, and song.[8] Of these, two parts are the means of imitation,
one is the manner of imitation, three are the objects of imitation,[9] and
there are no others. No small number of [dramatists], one might say,
have used these kinds [of parts], for all dramas are alike in having spectacle and character and plot and diction and song and *thought*.

Now the most important of these parts is the composition of the   15
events. For tragedy is an imitation not of men but of *action*[10] and a way
of life and happiness or unhappiness; for happiness and unhappiness,
too, exist in *action*, and the end of man is a kind of *action* and not a
quality.[11] Thus men are of a certain quality by virtue of their character, but they are happy or its contrary by virtue of their *actions*.   20
Hence performers act not in order to imitate character; they take on
character for the sake of [imitating] *actions*. Accordingly, the events
and the plot are the end in tragedy, and [in general] the end in each
thing is the most important [part].[12] Besides, without *action* tragedy
would not exist, but it would exist without character.[13] In fact, the   25
tragedies of most young poets are deficient in character, and in gen-

eral many poets are of this kind.[14] Such is the case, too, with painters,
e.g., Zeuxis in comparison with Polygnotus; for Polygnotus is a good
portrayer of character, but the painting of Zeuxis has no character at
all. Moreover, if someone were to set down in a drama a succession of
dramatic speeches which reveal [mainly] character and are well ex-
30   pressed in diction and *thought*, he would not perform what was stated
to be the function of tragedy; but a tragedy which, although employ-
ing these in a somewhat deficient way, has a plot and a composition of
events will achieve [the function of tragedy] far better. In addition,
the greatest [elements] by which tragedy moves the soul—reversals
35   and recognitions[15]—are parts of the plot. Another sign of this point is
the fact that those who attempt to write tragedy are able to be accurate in diction and in the portrayal of character before they are able to
construct the events [well],[16] and such was the case with almost all the
early poets.

The plot, then, is the principle and, as it were, the soul of tragedy;[17]
1450*b*   character comes second.[18] In fact, there is a parallel even in painting; if
some artist were to lay on the finest colors without order, he would not
delight the viewer as well as the artist who sketches a likeness of an object in black and white.[19] Tragedy, after all, is an imitation of *action*;
and it is an imitation of agents for the sake of that *action* most of all.

5   Third [in order of importance] is *thought*, that is, the ability to express what there is to be said and what is fitting, and to speak in this
manner is the function of politics and rhetoric.[20] In fact, the early
poets made their agents speak like statesmen, whereas the poets nowadays make them speak like rhetoricians. Now character in speech is
the kind of quality which makes clear the speaker's intention; and in
general, for just this reason, speeches which do not reveal whether
10   the speaker intends to pursue or avoid doing something have no
character.[21] *Thought*, on the other hand, is found in those speeches in
which speakers (a) argue that something is or is not the case, or (b) express something universally.

Fourth is diction in language; by "diction," as mentioned before,[22] I
mean the manner in which meaning is expressed in words;[23] and this
15   part has the same effect whether in verse or in prose. Of the remaining
parts, the fifth, which is the use of song, is the most pleasing accessory.
As for [the sixth part], the spectacle, although it moves the soul, it is of
all the parts the least a matter of art and has the least to do with the art
of poetry; for the effect of [a good] tragedy is possible even without

performance or performers. Besides, the working out of the spectacle
comes under stagecraft more than under the art of the poet.   20

7   beginning - middle - end

   These matters having been specified, let us next discuss the kind of
structure which the events should have, since this is the first and most
important part of tragedy. We have posited that tragedy is an imita-   25
tion of *action*[1] that is complete and a whole and has a certain magnitude; for a thing may be a whole even if it has no magnitude.[2] Now
that which has a beginning and a middle and an end is a whole. A beginning is that which may come but not of necessity after another
thing, but another thing comes by its nature into existence or is generated after it;[3] an end, on the contrary, is that which by its nature
comes after another thing, either of necessity or for the most part, but 30
no other thing comes after it; and a middle is that which [by its nature]
comes after something else and precedes another thing. Well-
structured plots, therefore, should not begin at any chance [event]
nor end at any chance [event] but should use the ideas just stated.
   Furthermore, that which is beautiful, whether an animal or any
other thing which is composed of a number of parts, should have not   35
only these parts [properly] ordered but also a magnitude, and not any
chance magnitude. Indeed, beauty exists in magnitude as well as in
order;[4] for this reason, neither could a tiny animal become beautiful
(for our view of it, which takes place in an almost imperceptible interval of time, becomes blurred), nor could an animal of very large size   1451*a*
(for the visual grasp of it and of its parts does not take place simultaneously, so its unity and wholeness are lost for the viewer, e.g., if there
were to be an animal a thousand miles long). Hence, just as the magnitude of an inanimate body or of an animal should be such as to be easily visible [as a whole], so the length of a plot should be such as can be   5
easily retained in memory. As for the proper limit of a plot's length, if
related to the performance at dramatic competitions and to [the
audience's] perception, it does not come under the dramatic art;[5] for
if a hundred tragedies had to compete, they would have to be timed
by water-clocks, as is said to have occurred at one time. The proper
limit of a [good tragedy or plot] according to its own nature is this: the 10
greater the length up to the limit of being grasped as a whole,[6] the
more beautiful it is with respect to its magnitude. Simply specified,
however, an adequate limit to the magnitude of the thing [i.e., the

plot] is such that, if the events occur in a sequence which is either
probable or necessary,[7] a change takes place [in the protagonist] from
15   misfortune to good fortune or from good fortune[8] to misfortune.

8   *unity: wholeness of the plot*

A plot has unity not [simply], as some suppose, if it is concerned
with a single [*man*]; for many or an indefinite number of generically
distinct things may happen [to a *man*], yet from some of them no unity
can be made. So, too, a *man* may perform many *actions* from which no
20   unity results. For this reason, all those poets who wrote a *Heracleid*, a
Theseid, and other such poems seem to have been mistaken. Such
poets think that, since Heracles was one *man*, the plot, too, must have
unity. But just as Homer excelled in other respects, either because of
his art or because of his nature,[1] so, too, he seems to have grasped this
25   point well; for in composing the *Odyssey*, [to take an example], he did
not include everything that had happened to Odysseus: Odysseus had
been wounded on Mount Parnassus and also had feigned madness at
the mustering of [Agamemnon's] army, but the latter event did not
follow from the former, whether of necessity or with [high]
probability.[2] He composed the *Odyssey* as a unified *action* of the kind
30   we have described,[3] and he did likewise with the *Iliad*. Just as in the
other imitative arts, then, a single imitation should be of a unified object, so the plot, too, being an imitation of *action*, should be an imitation of one *action* which is a whole, with events as parts so constructed
that the transposition or removal of any part will make the whole dif-
35   ferent or perturb it; for if the presence or absence of a thing [in a
whole] produces no distinguishable difference, that thing is not a part
of that whole.[4]

9

It is also evident from what has been said that the task of the poet is
to state, not what has [actually] occurred, but the kinds of things
which might [be expected to] occur, and these are possible by virtue
1451*b*   of their probability[1] or their necessity. In fact, the historian differs
from the poet not by stating things without rather than with meters—
the writings of Herodotus would be no less a history if they were produced with meter rather than without meter—but by speaking of
what has actually occurred, whereas the poet speaks of the kinds of
5   things which are likely to occur. In view of this, poetry is both more

philosophical and more serious than history; for poetry speaks rather ✳
of what is universally the case, whereas history speaks of particular
events which actually occurred. The kinds of things that a certain
kind of man happens to say or do in accordance with probability or
necessity are universal, and poetry aims at such things, albeit it at-   10
taches names [to individuals];[2] what Alcibiades actually did or suffered, on the other hand, is a particular.

   Now this practice has already become clear in comedy; for having
constructed the plot in accordance with what is probable, the comic
poets then proceed to assign chance names, unlike the lampooning
poets, who make their poems about a particular man. In tragedy, how-   15
ever, the poets stick to historic names; and the *reason* for this is that it
is the possible which is persuasive. We[3] are somehow not convinced
that things which have not occurred are possible;[4] but it is evident
that what has occurred is possible, for it would not have occurred had
it been impossible. And yet, even in some tragedies only one or two   20
names of individuals are familiar to the audiences and the rest are
made up;[5] and in other tragedies not even one name of an actual individual is well known, e.g., in the *Antheus* of Agathon, for in this play
both the events and the names of the agents are made up, and yet the
play delights us none the less. So one must not seek in every case to
stick to traditional plots, with which [most] tragedies are concerned;   25
indeed, to seek to do so would be ridiculous, seeing that even [the
names of] eminent men [in the past] are [nowadays] familiar only to a
few, and yet those tragedies delight everyone.

   It is clear from these statements, then, that the poet should be a
maker of plots rather than of meters, inasmuch as he is a poet by virtue of imitation and imitates *actions*.[6] So even if he happens to use   30
things that actually occurred, he is no less a poet; for nothing prevents
some past occurrences which he uses as a poet from being the kinds of
things that are probable and could happen again.[7]

   Without qualification,[8] of plots and *actions* the episodic are the
worst. By "episodic plot" I mean a plot in which it is neither probable   35
nor necessary for the episodes to follow one after the other.[9] Such
plots are produced by bad poets because of their own [lack of art], by
good poets because of the performers; for by making pieces for show
and by stretching the plot beyond its capability, [good poets] are often   1452a
compelled to distort the [necessary or probable] sequence of events.

   Now a tragic imitation is not only of a complete *action*, but also of

events which arouse fear and pity, and these events come about
best—and do so more when they occur unexpectedly—if they occur
5   because of each other. For they are more wonderful if they occur in
this manner rather than if they occur by *chance* or by luck.[10] And even
those which occur by luck are thought to be most wonderful if they
appear to occur as though by design, as in the case of the statue of
Mitys at Argos: while the man who caused the death of Mitys was
looking at the statue, it fell and killed him. Events such as these seem
10   to occur not without plan, and so plots [with such events] are of necessity finer [than plots with events which occur just by chance].

10

Of plots, some are simple and the others are complex; for the *actions* which plots imitate, too, are such to begin with. By "simple *ac-
15   tion*" I mean one in which, being continuous and having unity, as
already specified,[1] a change of fortune occurs without reversal or recognition; by "complex *action*" I mean one in which a change of fortune occurs with reversal or recognition or both. These [changes][2]
should come about from the very structure of the plot and so turn out
20   to be either necessary or probable consequences of the preceding
events; for what occurs *because* of preceding events is far different
from what occurs [merely] *after* preceding events.[3]

11

A reversal, as has been mentioned,[1] is a change of things being done
to a contrary [from what is expected], and this [change], as we have
been saying, [should come about] in accordance with what is probable
25   or necessary. Thus in the *Oedipus [Rex*, the messenger] who came to
cheer up Oedipus and to rid him of his fear about his relation with his
mother produced the contrary effect when he revealed who Oedipus
really was;[2] and in the *Lynceus*, when Lynceus was led away to die and
Danaus followed in order to kill him, it turned out, as a consequence
of what had been done, that Danaus died and Lynceus was saved.
30   Recognition, as the name itself signifies, is a change from ignorance
to knowledge resulting in either friendship or enmity towards those
who are marked for good fortune or misfortune; and the finest recognition is the one which occurs at the same time as the reversal, like the
one in the *Oedipus [Rex]*.[3] But recognitions may be of other kinds
also; for recognition of someone may occur through an inanimate or

an animate chance [cause], as just stated,[4] or through the fact that   35
someone did or did not do something. But the kind of recognition
most [proper] to the plot and to the *action* is the one first mentioned:
it is the kind which, along with a reversal, will arouse either pity or
fear; for tragedy, as imitation, has been posited[5] as being of *actions*   1452*b*
which arouse pity or fear. Besides, bad or good fortune will follow in
such cases. Now since this recognition occurs between men, in some
cases only one of them is recognized by the other, and this occurs
whenever the identity of the latter is already known; in other cases   5
each must recognize the other, e.g., Iphigenia was recognized by
Orestes from the letter that was sent, but a second recognition, in
which Orestes is made known to Iphigenia, was needed.

Two parts of [a complex] plot, then, are reversal and recognition; a   10
third part is suffering. Of these, the first two have been discussed. As
for suffering, it is an *action* which tends to lead to destruction or distress, e.g., to death on stage, agony, wounds, and the like.

12

We have discussed previously the parts which give a tragedy its   15
quality,[1] but the separate parts into which a tragedy as a quantity is divided are as follows: prologue, episode, exode, and choral song, the
parts of the last being the parode and the stasimon.[2] Now these [parts]
are common to every [tragedy], but certain other parts are proper to
some [tragedies], namely, the [songs] from the stage[3] and the
commoi.[4] The prologue is the whole part of a tragedy which precedes   20
the parode, [i.e., the entrance of the chorus]; the episode is the whole
part of a tragedy that comes between [two] whole choral songs; the
exode is the whole part of a tragedy after which there is no choral
song. As for the choral parts, the parode is the first utterance, taken as
a whole, of the chorus; then the stasimon is a choral song without anapests or trochees; finally, the *commos* is a lamentation sung in common by the chorus and the performers from the stage.   25

The parts which a tragedy should use, then, are those [i.e., the qual-
itative] which were discussed earlier and the quantitative, which have
just been stated.

13

After what has been said,[1] we should discuss next those things at
which tragic poets should aim and those which they should guard

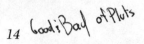
30 against in constructing their plots, and also the things from which the tragic function will be achieved.[2]

Now the construction of the finest tragedy should be complex and not simple,[3] and such tragedy should imitate *actions* which arouse fear and pity (for this is the proper function of such imitation). It

35 clearly follows, then, that (1) neither should fair–minded *men* be shown changing from good fortune to misfortune, for this change arouses neither fear nor pity but is repugnant;[4] (2) nor should wicked *men* be shown changing from bad fortune to good fortune, for this change is the most untragic of all, inasmuch as it has none of the ef-

1453*a* fects it should have, since it arouses no compassion and neither pity nor fear;[5] and (3) nor should an utterly worthless *man* undergo a fall from good fortune to misfortune, for a tragedy thus constructed might arouse compassion but neither pity nor fear, inasmuch as pity is

5 aroused by the misfortune of one who does not deserve it and fear by the misfortune of one who is like us, in which case the outcome of such construction will arouse neither pity nor fear.[6] The remaining type, then, lies between these two; and such is the *man* who, not dif-fering [from us][7] in virtue and in justice,[8] and being one of those who

10 have a great reputation[9] and good fortune, changes to misfortune not because of vice or wickedness but because of some error,[10] as in the case of Oedipus and Thyestes and other famous *men* from families of this sort.

It is necessary, then, that a good plot be not double, as some say, but rather single [in its outcome][11] and change not from misfortune to

15 good fortune but, on the contrary, from good fortune to misfortune, not because of wickedness but because of some grave error[12] commit-ted either by the sort of *man* we have cited or by one who is better than average rather than worse.[13] A sign of this is what has happened [in the history of the theater]; for at first the poets would recount any story that came their way, but now the finest tragedies are composed

20 about a few families, e.g., those of Alcmaeon, Oedipus, Orestes, Meleager, Thyestes, Telephus, and others who have happened to do or suffer terrible things. The finest tragedy according to the poetic art, then, arises from a construction of this kind; and it is for this rea-son that those who criticize severely Euripides for using this [princi-

25 ple] and ending many of his tragedies in misfortune are mistaken, for this [type of ending] is, as we have said, the right one. But the best sign of this fact is the following: if such tragedies are rightly executed on

the stage and in [dramatic] competitions, they turn out to be the most tragic;[14] and Euripides, even if he does not manage other things well,[15] still appears to be the most tragic of the poets. 30

In second rank is the kind of composition which some say comes first, namely, that which has a double construction, like the *Odyssey*, and has contrary endings for the better and for the worse agents.[16] Such tragedy is thought to be first in rank because of the weakness of audiences, for the poets go along with the desires of the spectators.[17] This pleasure is 35 not tragic[18] but rather appropriate to comedy; for, in a comedy, the bitterest enemies in the plot, such as Orestes and Aegisthus, go off as friends at the end and nobody is killed by anybody.[19]

14

Now it is possible that what arouses fear and pity come from the 1453*b* spectacle, but it is also possible that these feelings come from the very structure of the events;[1] and indeed this is a better[2] imitation and a mark of a better poet. For the plot should be so constructed as to make the one hearing the events shudder[3] and feel pity as a result of 5 what happens, even without seeing the tragedy performed. Such indeed is what anyone would feel on hearing the plot of the *Oedipus [Rex]*. To produce this effect by means of spectacle is less a matter of art and requires extraneous apparatus.[4] As for those who, by means of spectacle, produce not a fearful sight but only a monstrous one, they 10 are not dealing with tragedy; for one should seek to arouse from tragedy not every kind of pleasure but only that which is appropriate to it. So, since the poet should produce through imitation the kind of pleasure that comes from pity and fear, it is evident that he must do so by means of the events themselves. Let us, then, take up what sort of encounters appear terrible or grievous. 15

Such *actions* must be directed towards those who are either friends or enemies or neither. Now if someone kills or is about to kill an enemy, [the *action*], whether performed or about to be performed, does not arouse pity, except for the suffering itself; and this is the case even if [the agent] is neither a friend nor an enemy of the victim.[5] But whenever the sufferings occur among friends, e.g., if a brother kills or 20 is about to kill or do some other such thing to his brother, or a son his father, or a mother her son, or a son his mother, these are what the tragic poet should look for.[6] The tragic poet, then, need not disturb the traditional stories (I mean, for example, the death of

Clytaemnestra at the hand of Orestes and that of Eriphyle at the hand
25 of Alcmaeon), but he should devise incidents and handle the traditional material well.[7] Let us state more clearly what we mean by the
term "well."

It is possible to make the *action* occur as the older poets did, that is,
by making the agents know what they are doing and to whom they are
doing it, e.g., as Euripides does in making Medea kill her children.[8] It
30 is also possible to have the agents *act* but be ignorant of the terrible
deed done and later recognize the kinship, as Sophocles does in his
Oedipus [Rex]. Here the deed occurs outside the drama; but the deed
may be in the tragedy itself, e.g., the *act* of Alcmaeon in Astydamas'
tragedy or of Telegonus in *The Wounded Odysseus*.[9] There is also a
35 third way, one in which the agent, being about to perform an irrepara-
ble deed not knowing the true identity of the intended victim, recognizes him before he does it. There are no other possible ways; for the
agent must either *act* or not *act*, and he either knows or does not know
toward whom he is about to *act*.

The worst of these possibilities is the one in which the agent is
about to *act* knowing toward whom he is to *act* but fails to *act*; for this
action is repugnant and, being devoid of suffering, has no tragic ef-
1454a fect. For this reason, no one uses this possibility or one does so rarely,
as in *Antigone*, in which Haemon [threatens to kill his father Creon,
but does not]. The second possibility is one in which the agent [knows
and] *acts*. There is a [third and] better way, one in which the agent *acts*
in ignorance and then recognizes what he has done, for there is noth-
5 ing repugnant here and the recognition is striking. The best of all is
the remaining.[10] In the *Cresphontes*, for example, Merope is about to
kill her son but, recognizing him, does not do so;[11] in the *Iphigenia*,
the sister recognizes her brother and does not kill him;[12] and in the
Helle, the son, about to hand over his mother [to the enemy], recognizes her [and does not do so].[13] It is for this *reason*, as stated earlier,
10 that the [existing] tragedies are concerned with only a few families;[14]
for the [earlier] poets, in looking for [tragic material], discovered by
luck and not by art [the way to] produce such [a tragic effect] in their
plots,[15] and [even now] poets [still] find it necessary to have recourse
to those [few] houses in which such sufferings occurred.[16]

Concerning the structure of events and the kinds of plots which
15 tragedies should have, then, enough has been said.

15 characters

Concerning character, there are four things at which the poet should aim. (1) The foremost is that it should be cogent.[1] Now an agent will have [cogent] character if, as stated previously,[2] his words and *actions* make evident his intentions; so his character will not be cogent if his intentions are not made evident but will be cogent if his intentions are made evident. But [cogency of character] depends on the role of the agent. A woman and a slave, too, may be [portrayed] cogently, [but in a different manner]; for perhaps a woman is inferior[3] to a *man*, whereas a slave is of no account at all.[4] (2) The character should fit the agent; for [a *man*] may be [portrayed as] manly in character, but it is not fitting to portray a woman as being manly or shrewd.[5] (3) The character should be similar[6] [to those we find in life]; for this is distinct from making character cogent or fitting as we have just described. (4) The character should be consistent; and even if the character is portrayed as being inconsistent, it should nevertheless be portrayed as being *consistently* inconsistent.

An example of baseness of character which is not necessary is that of Menelaus in the *Orestes*;[7] of what is improper and unfitting [examples are] Odysseus' lamentation in the *Scylla* and Melanippe's speech;[8] and of inconsistency [an example is] the character in *Iphigenia at Aulis*, for Iphigenia the suppliant in no way resembles her later self.[9]

In portraying character, too, as in constructing the events, the poet should always look for what is either necessary or probable, so as to have a given agent speak or *act* either necessarily or probably, and [hence] to have one event occur after another either necessarily or probably.[10] It is evident, then, that the resolutions of the plots, too, should come about from the plot itself[11] and not by the use of *deus ex machina*,[12] as in the *Medea*, or in the stampede of the Greeks in the *Iliad*. This device should be used [if at all] for events outside the drama,[13] either those in the past which cannot be known by man, or those in the future which require foretelling and reporting; for it is to the gods that we attribute the power of seeing all things. Again, there should be nothing unreasonable in the events, or, if there is, it should be outside the tragedy, as in the case of the *Oedipus [Rex]* of Sophocles.[14]

Since a tragedy is an imitation of men who are better than average,[15] tragic poets should follow the example of good portrait

10   painters; for, in painting men, they represent them more beautifully
     than they are but still retain the likeness of their visible form. So, too,
     when the poet imitates men who are quick or slow to anger or who
     have other such [defects of] character, he should render them as ex-
     amples of fair–minded or indignant men, as Agathon and Homer
     made Achilles.[16]
15   The poet, then, should keep in mind these points and, in addition,
     the stage effects on the audience which must conform to the poetic
     art; for it is often possible to make mistakes here also.[17] But these mat-
     ters have been sufficiently discussed in our published treatises.[18]

         16 – *recognition through sign*

20   What recognition is has been stated earlier;[1] let us turn to its kinds.
         Recognitions of the first kind are those through signs, and these are
     the most inartistic but most often used by poets because of their lack
     of resourcefulness. Some signs are congenital, as in "the lance which
     the earthborn bear on their [bodies]"[2] or the kind of 'stars' used in the
25   *Thyestes* by Carcinus.[3] Other signs are acquired after birth; and of
     these, some are bodily, like scars, others are external tokens, such as
     necklaces or the little boat which led to the recognition in the *Tyro*.
     And it is possible to use these in a better or worse way; for example,
     Odysseus was recognized by his scar in one way by his nurse, in an-
     other way by his swineherds. Recognitions which use signs for the
     sake of convincing others—indeed all such recognitions—are rather
30   inartistic; those which arise from reversal are better, like the one in
     the Bath Scene [in the *Odyssey*].[4]
         Of the second kind are those devised by the poet; and for this rea-
     son they are inartistic. One example is the manner in which Orestes
     reveals himself in *Iphigenia in Tauris*: he recognizes his sister by the
     letter, then he reveals himself by saying what the poet wants him to
35   say and not what the plot requires.[5] For this reason the mistake [in the
     poetic art] is somewhat similar to that mentioned above, for Orestes
     could just as well have brought some [tokens]. The Voice of the Shut-
     tle in the *Tereus* of Sophocles is another example.[6]
1455*a*   Third is the recognition through memory, when at the sight of an
     object one is affected in some way; in the *Cyprians* of Dicaeogenes,
     for example, a man bursts into tears at the sight of a picture. And in
     The Tale of Alcinous we have another example: Odysseus, hearing the

minstrel play the lyre and remembering the past, weeps and, as a result, is recognized.[7]

Fourth is the recognition from inference. For example, in the *Choephoroi* we have the following: "Someone resembling me has come; nobody resembles me except Orestes; therefore it is Orestes who has come."[8] We have another example [proposed] by the sophist Polyidus for *Iphigenia*: it would be probable for Orestes to reason thus, "My sister was sacrificed at the altar, and now I, too, am to be sacrificed."[9] So, too, in the *Tydeus* of Theodectes, the father says, "I came to find my son, and I am to perish myself."[10] Again, the women in the *Phineidae*,[11] having seen the place, inferred their destiny: "Here we are destined to die, for here we were cast forth." There is also a composite recognition arising from false reasoning on the part of the audience, as in *Odysseus the False Messenger*; for [Odysseus] says that he will know the bow (which he actually had not seen), but the listener commits the fallacy of thinking that he will be recognized [by that statement].[12]

The best of all recognitions is that which arises from the events themselves, when the striking effect comes through probabilities, such as that which we find in the *Oedipus [Rex]* of Sophocles;[13] another appears in *Iphigenia [in Tauris]*, (725–803), for it is probable that Iphigenia should wish to be sending letters home.[14] Such recognitions are the only ones that occur without the use of contrived signs or amulets. The next best are the recognitions which arise from inference.

17

In constructing the plot and in working out the diction to go with it, the poet should make it his special effort to set the scene as vividly as possible before his eyes; for in this way, visualizing as distinctly as possible the events just as if he were a spectator of the performers in *action*, he would discover what is proper and so be least likely to overlook incongruities.[1] A sign of this is [the mistake] for which Carcinus was censured. [The plot requires that] Amphiaraus [be seen] returning from the temple; but his return, not seen [on stage], was not evident to the audience, and the play failed in performance, since the spectators were displeased by this [oversight].[2]

Further, the poet should work out the plot by making the appropriate gestures himself as far as possible. Men are most persuasive whose sufferings are brought about naturally;[3] for those who show agitation or

anger most truly are those who are actually agitated or angry.[4] It is in
view of this that the poetic art belongs to those who are naturally gifted
or who have a touch of madness; for the former easily mold themselves
to any emotion, whereas the latter are prone to ecstatic [empathy].[5]

1455b   As for the story, whether the poet takes it as handed down or makes
it up himself, he should make an outline of it, and then on this basis
make up episodes and fill in details.[6] What I mean by "an outline," to
take *Iphigenia [in Tauris]* as an example, is the following: a certain
maiden, being offered up in sacrifice, disappears mysteriously from
the presence of those who are sacrificing her; being settled in another
5   country, in which it was the custom to sacrifice strangers to the god-
dess [Artemis], she is made the priestess. Sometime later, the brother
[Orestes] of the priestess happens to come to this country (the fact
that the god for some *reason* told him through an oracle to go there
and what he commanded him to do is entirely outside the plot). Upon
10   his arrival he is seized; and, as he is about to be sacrificed, he is recognized, whether as Euripides brings it about or as Polyidus does by
making him say, as it was probable that he would, "So not only my sister but I, too, must be sacrificed." As a result, he is saved.[7] Once the
names of the agents have been assigned, the poet should then make
up the episodes and see to it that they are appropriate. In the case of
Orestes, for example, one such episode is Orestes' fit of madness
15   which led to his capture, another is the rite of purification which led
to his salvation.

Now the episodes in a drama are short; an epic poem, however, is
lengthened by longer episodes, yet its outline is not long, as in the
Odyssey: a certain man has been away from home for many years, kept
that way by Poseidon, and he ends up being alone. Meanwhile, his af-
20   fairs at home are in such a state that his wife's suitors are squandering
his property and are plotting against his son. Tempest–tossed, he ar-
rives home; he reveals himself to some; he attacks and destroys his enemies and is saved. That is the essence[8] of the *Odyssey*; the rest is
made up of episodes.

18

One part of every tragedy is complication, the other is resolution.[1]
25   Events outside [the drama], and often some of those within it, constitute the complication, while the remaining part constitutes the resolution. By "complication"[2] I mean the part from the beginning[3] until

the last part after which a change from good fortune to bad ... fortune[4] occurs; and by "resolution" I mean the part from the beginning of this change until the end. Thus, in the *Lynceus* of Theodectes, 30 the complication consists of the events that occurred before [the tragedy starts], the seizure of the child, ... [and also that of the parents];[5] the resolution is the part from the accusation of murder until the end.

There are four species [or kinds] of tragedy, for, as mentioned previously, there are as many parts: (1) the complex tragedy, the whole of it consisting of reversal and recognition; (2) the tragedy of suffering, such as those that deal with Ajax and Ixion; (3) the tragedy of charac- 1456*a* ter, e.g., the *Phthiotides* and *Peleus*; and (4) ... [...], such as the *Phorcides* and the *Prometheus* and those which are about Hades.[6]

Now the poet should do his utmost to work out well all the [parts], or at least most of them and the most important ones, especially nowa- 5 days when critics carp at poets. In the past, each part was well worked out by some poets, but nowadays a poet is expected to surpass each of the older poets at his special excellence.

It is also just to speak of tragedies as being the same or different with respect to the plot more than to any other part; and by "having the same plot" we mean tragedies whose involvements[7] and resolutions are the same.[8] Yet many poets work out the involvement well but 10 the resolution poorly; but both should always be mastered.

Again, one must keep in mind what has often been said[9] and not try to make a tragedy out of an epic structure (and by "epic structure" here I mean one with many plots), e.g., not to make a tragic plot out of the whole of the *Iliad*. In epic, the parts assume a suitable magnitude because of the epic's length, but in drama, [the use of episodes suit- 15 able for one epic] goes far beyond what is expected. A sign of this is that the poets who have made a tragedy by using the whole capture of Troy instead of a part of it, as did Euripides, or the whole story of Niobe instead of a part of it, as did Aeschylus, either failed or showed up badly in the competitions; and even Agathon failed once in this respect. In reversals and in simple events,[10] however, [these poets] suc- 20 ceed remarkably well in achieving what they wish. For the effect produced is tragic or else it arouses a feeling of compassion, as in the case of a clever rogue like Sisyphus, who is outwitted, or of a brave but unjust man who is defeated.[11] As Agathon says, an event of this kind has a probability of occurring, since [according to him] improbable things, too, have a [mathematical] probability of occurring.[12] 25

The chorus, too, should be regarded as one of the performers, as a part of the whole and as sharing in the *action*, that is, not in the manner of Euripides, but in that of Sophocles.[13] As for the choral songs [of the later poets], they are no more parts of the plots [of their tragedies] than [of the plot] of any other tragedy; and for this reason they are 30 [nowadays] sung as interludes—a practice first introduced by Agathon. But, one may ask, what difference is there between singing choral parts as interludes and fitting a speech or a whole episode from one tragedy into another?

19

Now that [plot and character] have been discussed, it remains to take up diction and *thought*.[1]
35   Concerning *thought*, let the discussion of it in the *Rhetoric*[2] be assumed here,[3] for this topic is more proper to that *inquiry*.[4] The things concerned with *thought* [in tragedy] are all those matters which should be rendered by speech; and the parts of these[5] are (a) demon-
1456b   strating and refuting, (b) rendering the feelings, such as pity, fear, anger, and the like, and also (c) maximizing or minimizing what is to be said.[6] In dealing with events [occurring on stage], too, it is clear that the poet should use the same devices[7] as those he uses for *thought* in presenting those events as pitiful or terrible or important 5   or probable [or etc.],[8] but with this difference: whereas things spoken should be presented by or follow from the speaker's choice, [actual events on stage] should be apparent without any verbal exposition.[9] For what else would the speaker add to those events if they were to appear [on stage] as they should without any verbal exposition?
    Of the [parts] concerned with diction, one kind of inquiry deals 10   with the forms of diction, such as what an injunction is, a prayer, a narration,[10] a threat, a question, an answer,[11] and others like them, and understanding of these comes under the [science] of delivery or under one who has the architectonic [science] which includes the [science] of delivery. No serious censure, then, should be directed to one's [poetic] art for his knowledge or ignorance about these matters. 15   For example, why would anyone regard as a [poetic] mistake that which Protagoras censures: that Homer, meaning to pray, used a command when he said "Sing, Goddess, the wrath ...?" For Protagoras says that telling someone to do or not to do something is a command.

For this reason, let us pass over this study as belonging not to poetics but to another [science].

20

The [material] parts of diction in general are as follows: letters, syllables, connectives, nouns, verbs, joints, inflections, and speech.[1]   20

Now a letter is an indivisible vocal sound, not any such sound but one from whose nature, as a part, a composite[2] vocal sound can be formed; for brutes, too, can make indivisible vocal sounds, but I do not call any of these "a letter." The kinds of letters are the vowel, the   25 semivowel, and the mute.[3] A vowel, such as "a" and "o," is a letter having an audible vocal sound without the application [of the tongue or lips or teeth to the various parts of the mouth]. A semivowel, such as "s" and "r," is a letter having an audible vocal sound[4] made with the application [of the tongue or lips or teeth, etc.]. A mute, such as "g" and "d," is a letter formed with the application [of the tongue or lips or teeth, etc.] and has no vocal sound by itself; but, when combined   30 with letters having vocal sound, it becomes audible.[5] Letters differ with respect to the shapes assumed by the mouth and with respect to the places [at which they are formed], and they are (a) aspirated or unaspirated, (b) long or short, and (c) acute or grave or intermediate [in pitch].[6] Each of these comes under the [science] that is concerned with metrical matters.

A syllable is a non–significant vocal sound composed of a mute and   35 a letter having vocal sound; thus "gr" without the vowel "a" is a syllable, and so is "gra," which has the vowel "a." But the discussion of these distinctions, too, belongs to [the science of] metrics.[7]

A connective is (a) a non–significant vocal sound which by its nature   1457a neither prevents nor produces a unity of a significant vocal sound composed of many vocal sounds, and which can be placed at either end or in the middle of a sentence unless its nature is such as it is not fitting to be placed at the beginning of a sentence, e.g., μέν, ἤ, τοι, δέ; or (b) a non–significant vocal sound which by its nature produces a unified sig-   5 nificant vocal sound out of more than one significant vocal sound.[8]

A joint is (a) a non–significant vocal sound which makes clear the beginning or end or dividing–point of a sentence, e.g., ["around"] or ["about"] and other such words; or, it is (b) a non–significant vocal sound which neither prevents nor produces a unified significant vocal

sound (i.e., a vocal sound composed of more than one vocal sound) and
10   by its nature can be placed at either end or in the middle of a sentence.

A noun is a composite vocal sound with meaning which does not include time, and no part of it by itself has meaning. In [some] double
nouns, too, each part considered not by itself but as a part has no
meaning; e.g., in the name "Fairbanks" the parts "Fair" and "banks"
have no meaning [as parts].⁹

A verb is a composite vocal sound having meaning which also in-
15   cludes time; and, just as with nouns, no part of it by itself has meaning. For the nouns "man" and "white" do not include time in their
meaning; but the verbs "walks" and "walked" include in their meanings present and past time, respectively, [in addition to the meaning of
the noun "walk."]¹⁰

An inflection is a modification of a noun or a verb and signifies: (a) a
20   genitive or dative or some other such [case], as in "of a house" or "to a
house," respectively; or (b) a singular or a plural, as in "man" and
"men," respectively; or (c) a form of delivery, as in a question raised or
a command given, for "Walked?" and "Walk!" are inflections of a verb
in accordance with these two kinds of mood.

Speech is a composite significant sound some parts of which, taken
25   by themselves, signify something. But not every speech consists of
nouns and verbs; for speech may have no verb, as in the definition of
man.¹¹ In any case, speech will always have a part which, taken by itself, signifies something;¹² e.g., the part "Cleon" in "Cleon walks" signifies something. Speech has unity in two ways: (a) if it signifies
something which is a unity, or (b) if it signifies a unity made by con-
30   necting many [speeches each of which has unity]. For example, the *Iliad* has unity by connection, whereas the definition of man has unity
by signifying just one thing.

21

Of the kinds of names,¹ some are simple (and by "simple" I mean a
name consisting of parts no one of which is significant, such as the
noun "hug"),² others are double; and some double names consist of
two parts, one significant and the other non–significant,³ but others
consist of [two] significant parts.⁴ There may also exist names which
35   are triple or quadruple or any other multiple, as we find many of them
in grandiloquent language, e.g., such as "megalomaniacology."⁵

Every name is either standard or foreign or metaphorical or orna-   1457*b*
mental or newly–coined or lengthened or shortened or altered.

By "standard" I mean a name that a group of men ordinarily use; by
"foreign" I mean one that is ordinarily used by other groups. So it is
evident that the same name may be both foreign and standard, but not   5
to the same group; for "*sigynon*" [= "lance"] is standard among the
Cyprians but foreign to us [the Athenians].

A metaphor is a name belonging to one thing but applied to another
thing, and it replaces (a) a genus of it, or (b) a species of it, or (c) another species [under the same genus], or (d) a thing analogous to it.⁶

An example of (a) is "There stood my ship," for "lying at anchor" is   10
a species of "standing." An example of (b) is "Truly Odysseus has done
ten thousand noble deeds," for "ten thousand" is a species of "many"
and is used here instead of "many." Examples of (c) are "drawing off
the soul with a bronze weapon" and "cutting away the blood with un-
yielding bronze"; for here the poet has used "drawing off" for "cut-   15
ting away" in the first example and "cutting away" for "drawing off" in
the second, and these two are species of "taking away."

By "analogy" I mean a similarity of relations in which A is to B as C
is to D. Here (a) the poet will use C instead of A or A instead of C; and
sometimes (b) the poet adds something related to the term used. I   20
mean, for example, that (a) the cup [A] is to Dionysus [B] as the shield
[C] is to Ares [D]; accordingly, the poet will call the cup "the shield of
Dionysus" and the shield "the cup of Ares." Or, again, old age is to life
as evening is to day; accordingly, the poet will speak of evening as
"the old age of day," and of old age as the "evening of life" or (as
Empedocles puts it) "the sunset of life." In some analogies, there is no   25
single name to signify one of the terms, but one may nevertheless
speak analogously. For example, the scattering of seed [by man] is
called "sowing," but there is no name for the emission of flame [by the
sun];⁷ still, this emission of flame is to the sun as sowing the seed is to
man, and for this reason, (b) the poet, [speaking of the sun], said "sowing the God–created flame." There is yet another way of using this   30
kind of metaphor: (c) the poet, in calling an object by a name belonging to another object, may then deny a predicate which is appropriate
to the name he uses; for example, he may call the shield not "the cup
of Ares" but "the wineless cup [of Ares]."⁸

A newly–coined name is one that is not used at all by any group of
men but is introduced by the poet himself; and some names are

35   thought to be of this sort, e.g., "sprouters" for "horns" and
      "supplicator" for "priest."[9]

1458a   A name may be either lengthened or shortened: it is said to be length-
      ened if a vowel longer than the appropriate vowel is used or if a syllable is
      inserted, e.g., if *"polēos"* is used for *"polĕos"* or *"Pelēiadeo"* for

5   *"Pelēidou"*; it is said to be shortened if something is taken away, e.g., if
      "kri" is used [instead of *"krithe"* (= "barley")] or *"dō"* [instead of *"dōma"*
      (= "house" or "chamber")], or *"ops"* [instead of *"opsis"* (= "vision")], as
      in *"mia ginetai amphoteron ops"* (= "a single vision sees both").

      A name is said to be altered whenever one part of the original is left
      unchanged but another part is made up, e.g., the poet uses *"dexiteron"*
      instead of *"dexion"* (= "to the right") in *"dexiteron kata mazon"*.[10]

      Some nouns are masculine, some feminine, and some in between
      [i.e., neuter]. Masculine nouns end in ν or ρ or ς [in English, "n" or "r"

10   or "s"] or in letters which include ς [="s"]; there are two of these, ψ [=
      "ps"] and ξ [= "ks"]. Feminine nouns end in vowels which are always
      long, i.e., in η̄ (= "e") and ω̄ (= "o") and in long ᾱ (= "ā"); thus the
      feminine endings are as many in number as the masculine, for the
      masculine endings ψ and ξ are really endings in "s." No noun ends in a

15   mute or a short vowel. Only three nouns end in ι (= "i"): *"meli"* (=
      "honey"), *"kommi"* (= "gum"), and *"peperi"* (= "pepper"), and only
      five end in υ (= "y"), *"pōy,"* *"nāpy,"* *"gony,"* *"dory,"* and *"asty,"* and
      neuter nouns end in these and in "n" or "s."

      22 .ux ot language

      It is a virtue of diction to be lucid without being commonplace.
      Now the most lucid kind of diction is the one that uses only standard

20   names, but such diction is commonplace; and examples of it are the
      poetry of Cleophon[1] and of Sthenelus.[2] Diction which uses strange [as
      well as standard] names,[3] however, has dignity and avoids ordinary
      language; and by "strange names" I mean names which are foreign or
      metaphorical or lengthened or any of those which are not standard.[4]
      But if one were to use only names such as those,[5] the result would be

25   enigmatic or barbaric, enigmatic if the diction consists of metaphors,
      barbaric if it consists of foreign names. An enigmatic diction takes the
      form of a combination of expressions signifying [literally] an impossi-
      ble connection of [things or facts]. A combination of [standard] names
      cannot achieve this, but metaphors can, as in "I saw a man sticking

bronze on another man with fire"[6] and the like. If, on the other hand,   30
one uses [only] foreign names, the result becomes a barbarism.

[Poetic diction,] then, should use [an appropriate combination of]
the above [two kinds, standard and strange names]; for foreign names
and metaphors and ornaments and the other forms will prevent diction from becoming ordinary or commonplace, whereas the use of
standard names will produce lucidity. Not the least part contributing
to [poetic] diction that is lucid without being ordinary is the one   1458*b*
which uses expansions and contractions and alterations of [standard]
names; for, by deviating from what is standard and thus going beyond
what is customary, diction avoids becoming ordinary, but by partak-   5
ing of the customary, it becomes lucid.

Critics, then, who object to a style such as the above and ridicule a poet
for using it are not right. Euclid the Elder, for example, was not right in
maintaining that it is easy to write poetry if one is allowed to lengthen
names at will; and he caricatured such style in the following lines:

> Ἐπιχάρην εἶδον Μαραθῶνάδε βαδίζοντα   10
> "Epicharus I/saw on his/way going/Mar–a/–thon/ward."
>
> and
>
> οὐκ ἄν γ᾽ ἐράμενος τὸν ἐκείνου ἑλλέβορον
> "not loving his hellebore."

Now the ostentatious use[7] of such devices is ludicrous, but their
moderate use is appropriate to every part of diction; in fact the inappropriate and deliberate[8] use of metaphors and foreign names and of
the other forms of diction would produce the same ludicrous effect.   15
But consider how much difference the use of what is fitting makes in
the epics if different names are inserted in verse; if one substitutes
standard names for foreign names or metaphors or any other form of
diction, one would realize the truth of what we are saying. For example, Aeschylus and Euripides produced the same iambic line; but   20
Euripides changed only one word, using a foreign instead of the usual
standard name, and his line appears beautiful, that of Aeschylus commonplace. Aeschylus wrote in the *Philoctetes*,

> φαγέδαινα ἥ μου σάρκας ἐσθίει ποδός
> ="cancer, which eats the flesh of the foot,"

but Euripides replaces ἐσθίει (= "eats") with θοινᾶται (= "feasts on").[9]

25   On the other hand,[10] in the line

    νῦν δέ μ' ἐὼν ὀλίγος τε καὶ οὐτιδανὸς καὶ ἀεικής[11]
    ="Now I, being paltry and frail and unseemly,"

one might use standard names and say,

    νῦν δέ μ̓ ἐὼν μικρός τε καὶ ἀσθενικὸς καὶ ἀειδής
    ="Now I, being small and weak and ugly,"

or in

    δίφρον ἀεικέλιον καταθεὶς ὀλίγην τε τράπεζαν[12]
    ="Having set an unseemly chair and a paltry table,"

one might do likewise and say,

30   δίφρον μοχθηρὸν καταθεὶς μικράν τε τράπεζαν
    ="Having set a bad chair and a small table."

Again, one might change ἠιόνες βοόωσιν (= "the sea–coasts roar")[13] to ἠιόνες κράζουσιν (= "the sea–coasts scream").

Ariphrades, too, ridiculed the tragedians for using expressions that no one would use in conversation, e.g., δωμάτων ἄπο (= "from the houses away") instead of ἀπὸ δωμάτων ("away from the houses"), and σέθεν "of thine" instead of "your"), and ἐγὼ δέ νιν (= "and I her"),[14]

1459a and Ἀχιλλέως πέρι (= "Achilles about") instead of περὶ Ἀχιλλέως (= "about Achilles"), and other such expressions. It is indeed because all such expressions are not standard that they produce a diction which is not ordinary; but Ariphrades was not aware of this fact.

5   The proper use of each of the devices mentioned as well as of double and foreign names is important, but by far the most important is the use of metaphors. Indeed [the ability for metaphor] alone [of the above devices] cannot be acquired from others but is a sign of a gift endowed by nature;[15] for to make metaphors well is to perceive similarities in things.[16]

Double names are most fitting for dithyrambs;[17] foreign names for heroic poems; and metaphors for iambic poems. Also, all [the forms of diction] mentioned above are useful for heroic poems; but for iambic

10

poems whose diction is the most imitative, those names are fitting which one might also use in conversation, and such are standard and metaphorical and ornamental names.[18]

Concerning tragedy or imitative *action* [on the stage], then, let the 15 above discussion be sufficient.

23

As for narrative which imitates in meter,[1] it is clear that it should have its plots constructed dramatically,[2] just as in tragedies, and it should be concerned with a single *action* which is a whole and complete, with a beginning and a middle and an end, like a single animal, 20 which is a whole,[3] in order to produce its appropriate pleasure;[4] and its compositions should not be similar to the usual historical accounts, each of which must present not a single *action* but all the chance and unrelated events involving one or more men during a single period.[5] For just as the sea–battle at Salamis and the battle with the 25 Carthaginians in Sicily occurred at the same time without being related to the same end, so too sometimes events succeed one another but have no single end.[6] Yet, in constructing their plots, a good many poets do what historians[7] do. 30

As we have stated earlier,[8] in this respect, too, Homer would appear to have been divinely inspired in comparison with the other poets: he did not attempt to make a poem out of the whole Trojan War even though that war had a beginning and an end, for the plot would have become too big to be easily grasped as a whole; or, even if it were moderated in length, it would have become too complex in its variety of events.[9] What he did was to select one part of the whole and use 35 many episodes taken from the other parts, e.g., the Catalogue of Ships and other episodes which he interspersed in the poem. But other poets produce epics about one man or one period or one *action* 1459*b* with a multitude of parts, as did the authors of the *Cypria* and of *The Little Iliad*. So, whereas only one or two tragedies can be made out of the *Iliad* or the *Odyssey*, many can be made out of the *Cypria* and more than eight out of *The Little Iliad*, i.e., *The Awarding of Arms*, 5 *Philoctetes, Neoptolemus, Eurypylus, The Beggary, the Laconian Women, The Sack of Troy, The Departure of the Fleet*, and one may add *Sinon* and *The Trojan Women*.

24

Furthermore, epic poetry should have the same species[1] as tragedy, for there may be a simple epic, or a complex epic, or an epic of char-
10   acter, or an epic of suffering. Its parts, except for song and spectacle, should also be the same; for epic, too, should make use of reversals and recognitions and sufferings.[2] Again, the *thought* and diction in an epic should be of beautiful quality.[3] Homer was the first to use all of these and to do so adequately; for, of his [two] poems, the *Iliad* is sim-
15   ple in structure and portrays suffering, while the *Odyssey*, using recognitions throughout and portraying character, is complex.[4] In ad- dition, he has surpassed all epic poets in diction and *thought*.[5]

Epic poetry differs from tragedy in the length of its composition and in meter. Now with respect to its length, the limitation stated earlier[6] is adequate, for one should be able to grasp as a whole both
20   the beginning and the end; and this will be possible if epic composi- tions are shorter than those of the early poets and the length of each amounts to that of a number of tragedies presented for one hearing.[7] With respect to extending its length, however, epic poetry has a spe- cial advantage, and there is a *reason* for this: tragedy does not admit
25   of imitating many parts [i.e., episodes] which take place at the same time but only that part which takes place on stage with the perform- ers; but epic poetry, being narrative, can be made to represent simul- taneously many parts which, if appropriately related, can lengthen the poem. So this virtue of epic poetry contributes to its grandeur and
30   pleases the audience by varying their interest and representing a di- versity of episodes; for monotony of events soon produces boredom and causes tragedies to fail.

The heroic meter [i.e., the hexameter] was found by trial and error to be [most] fitting. If one were to produce a narrative imitation in any other meter, or in several meters, it would appear unsuitable; for the
35   heroic is the most stately and most impressive of the meters, and for this reason it admits most readily foreign names and metaphors, and thereby narrative imitation surpasses other kinds. The iambic
1460*a*   [trimeter] and the [trochaic] tetrameter, on the other hand, are appro- priate for motion, the latter for the dance, the former for *action*. Fur- thermore, it would be rather absurd if anyone were to combine these meters, as Chaeremon did. And in fact, no one else has ever produced a long poetic composition in any meter other than the heroic, for, as

we have already stated, nature herself teaches poets to choose the fitting meter.[8]

Homer, who is worthy of praise for many other things, is also the   5
only poet who is not ignorant of what part he should play in his own poems. For an epic poet should speak in his own person as little as possible, otherwise he fails to imitate to the extent that he fails to impersonate [the agents in the poem].[9] The other poets put themselves forward throughout [their poems] and imitate but little and seldom. Homer, on the other hand, after a brief introduction, immediately   10 brings on a *man* or a woman or some other agent having character and not just a speaker devoid of character.

Now poets should produce an effect of wonder in their tragedies; but it is the epic that admits most readily what defies reason. It is in this way that epic achieves the effect of wonder, because the reader does not actually see the man performing the *action*. For example, the   15 passage recounting the pursuit of Hector, in which the Greeks stand still and do not pursue while Achilles shakes his head to keep them away, would certainly appear ludicrous on stage, but this absurdity escapes notice in epic poems. Of course, what arouses wonder gives pleasure; and a sign of this is that everyone, when reporting events, adds something of his own with a mind to please the audience.[10]

It was Homer, most of all, who also taught other poets how falsehoods should be expressed [artistically], namely, by the use of falla-   20 cies. For, if A's existence or occurrence implies B's existence or occurrence, respectively, men suppose that, conversely, B's existence or occurrence implies A's existence or occurrence. This inference, of course, is false. Now if A's truth implies B's truth, but A happens to be false while B is true, one might falsely infer that A is true also; and it is because of knowing the truth of B's existence that our mind commits   25 the fallacy of thinking that A, too, exists.[11] There is an example of this fallacy in the Bath Scene of the *Odyssey*.[12]

Again, plausible impossibilities should be preferred to unpersuasive possibilities. Still [plots] should be constructed not of unreasonable parts but at best of parts which include nothing unreasonable. If this cannot be done, the unreasonable parts should be outside of the actual plot, as is Oedipus' not knowing how Laius died, and not within   30 the drama, as is the messengers' account of the Pythian Games in the *Electra* or, in *The Mysians*, the man who came from Tegea to Mysia without saying a word. To argue that the plot would have been spoiled

[without these incidents] is ridiculous, for such plots should not have
been constructed that way in the first place. If, however, the poet in-
35   troduces something but makes it appear more reasonable than it really is, it should be allowed, even if it is an absurdity. For example, the
unreasonable episode in the *Odyssey*, in which Odysseus is landed on
1460*b*   the shores [of Ithaca], would clearly be intolerable if it had been written by an inferior poet. As it is, the poet [Homer] hides the absurdity
by rendering it pleasing with his other good artistic touches.

The poet should elaborate the diction of his poem in the parts in
which there is no *action* but not in those which manifest character or
5   *thought*, for highly brilliant diction conceals both character and *thought*.

25

Concerning the number and nature of the types of problems that
might arise [in evaluating poetry] and the [*reasons* the poet might
offer for their] solutions,[1] these become evident if viewed from the
following perspectives.
10   Since the poet is an imitator, like a painter or any other maker of
likenesses, he must always imitate one of three [kinds of] objects: (a)
things such as they were or are, or (b) objects such as they are said or
thought [to be or to have been], or (c) objects such as they should be.[2]
All these objects are communicated in diction, in which there are
foreign names and metaphors and many other features of diction that
we grant the poet to use.[3]
Furthermore, what is right in the poetic art is not the same as in the
15   political or any other art.[4] Mistakes within the poetic art itself are of
two kinds: (a) essential and (b) accidental. If the poet has chosen to
imitate something but failed through lack of [artistic] ability, the mistake violates the [poetic] art itself [i.e., it is essential]; but if he chose
incorrectly by imitating, for example, a horse with both right legs
thrown forward or made a mistake or portrayed something impossible
20   in any of the other arts, e.g., in medicine or some other art, the mistake is not essential [but accidental].[5]
Those who examine censures which arise from problems [in
poems], then, should resolve them by using the above [principles].
(1) If the poet introduces an object which is impossible with respect
to his own art, he makes a mistake. But he is right in doing so, provided
25   that the end of the art be served; for the end is enhanced if such use of
the impossible makes the corresponding part or some other part of the

poem more striking. An example is the pursuit of Hector.[6] If, however, the end could have been served just as well or better without violation of the principles of any of the arts, the mistake is not justifiable; for, if possible, a poet should make no mistake at all.[7]

(2) Furthermore, what kind of mistake is it: one that violates the [poetic] art or one that is accidental to that art? For it is a lesser mistake if the poet does not know that the female deer has no horns than if he has imitated her badly.[8]

(3) If a poet is censured for not representing things truly, he may [with justice] reply, "Well, I have represented them as they should be." For example, Sophocles said that he imitated men as they should be but that Euripides imitated them as they are.[9]

(4) If a poet is censured for imitating things neither as they are nor as they should be, he may [with justice] reply, "This is the way men speak of things," as in matters concerning the gods. For perhaps it is better [to imitate them] neither in this manner [i.e., as they should be] nor truly, but rather, as Xenophanes remarked, "But people do not speak [of them truly or as they should be]."

(5) In other cases, the poet may reply, "It is not better, [things being what they are nowadays], but such was the case with the objects in the past," as in the passage concerning arms, [where Homer says], "The spears stood upright, their butt–spikes in the ground," for such was the custom in those days, just as it is even now among the Illyrians.

(6) As to whether something was well or not well expressed or done, one should investigate the problem by attending not only to whether the thing done or said was [itself] good or bad, but also to the man who performed the deed or spoke, or the man this man spoke to or *acted* upon, or to the time he did so, or to the instrument he used, or to his purpose in doing so (e.g., in order to bring about a greater good or to avoid a greater evil).[10]

(7) Criticism concerning diction should be answered by attending to the language used, e.g., whether the poet has used a foreign word in the line "First [he slew] the *oureas*," for perhaps by the word "*oureas*" the poet meant not the mules but the guards. And when Homer said of Dolon, "He was deformed," perhaps he meant not that his body was badly proportioned, but that his face was ugly, for the Cretans call a handsome face "well–formed." And in the line "Mix the drink *zoroteron*," Homer meant by "*zoroteron*" not stronger [as one mixes it for drunkards] but more quickly.[11]

30

35

1461*a*

5

10

15

(8) Things expressed metaphorically have been discussed. For example, Homer says "All the gods and men slept the whole night long," but at the same time he also adds, "Whenever he [Agamemnon] gazed at the field of Troy, [he marveled] at the din of flutes and pipes."[12]

20 Here, the word "all" is used metaphorically instead of the word "many," for "all" is a species of "many." And in the line "She alone partakes not [in the baths of Ocean"] the word "alone" is used metaphorically, for the term "the most widely known" is a species of the term "alone."[13]

(9) With respect to pronunciation, one may solve problems as Hippias of Thasos did in the phrase δίδομεν δέ οἱ (= "We give him"), [where he changes the accent and makes the words mean "We give to him," not "Give to him,"][14] and in the phrase τὸ μὲν οὗ καταπύθεται ὄμβρῳ (= "A part of it is not rotted by rain"), [where he substituted οὐ (= "not") for οὗ (= "of which") and made the line read "A part is not rotted" instead of "A part of which is rotted"].[15]

(10) Some problems can be solved by division [i.e., grouping the words differently], as in Empedocles' line

25   αἶψα δὲ θνήτ' ἐφύοντο τὰ πρὶν μάθον ἀθάνατα
      ζωρά τε πρὶν κέκρητο

"Suddenly things grew mortal that before had learned to be immortal, and things unmixed before mixed,"

[where the final clause may be punctuated in two ways: (a) "things unmixed, before mixed" or (b) "things unmixed before, mixed"].[16]

(11) Some problems can be solved by clarifying the ambiguity, as in the line

παρῴχηκεν δὲ πλέω νύξ [τῶν δύο μοιράων, τριτάτη δ'
ἔτι μοῖρα λέλειπται]

="More [of the two parts of the] night had passed, [a third part was still left.]"

The word πλέω (= "more") is ambiguous.[17]

(12) Some problems can be solved by appealing to customary

usage. Wine mixed with water is still called "wine," and by the same principle Homer was correct when he wrote

κνημὶς νεοτεύκτου κασσιτέροιο
="A greave of newly–wrought tin,"

[for the word "tin" here means an alloy of tin and copper]; and work-ers of iron are called χαλκέας (= "bronze–workers"), and by the same principle Homer calls Ganymede "Zeus's wine–server," although the   30
gods do not drink wine [but only nectar].[18] This last example might also be taken as a metaphor. Also, whenever a name is thought to give rise to an inconsistency, one should examine how many senses it might have in the passage. For example, in the passage

τῇ ῥ᾽ ἔσχετο χάλκεον ἔγχος
="There the bronze spear was held,"

among the possible meanings of "being checked there," one might best avoid the mistake by taking the meaning opposed to the one as-   35
sumed by the critics.[19] Or else, as Glaucon says, some critics make un-   1461b
reasonable presuppositions about the meaning of a name used by a poet and proceed to draw conclusions based on those meanings; and if they think that an inconsistency arises from these conclusions, they censure the poet as if he actually said what it seems to them that he said. This is the treatment given to the passage about Icarius; for the critics suppose him to be a Spartan, and so they suppose it to be ab-   5
surd that Telemachus did not meet him when he went to Sparta. But perhaps the truth is just as the Cephallenians claim, for they say that Odysseus took a Cephallenian wife and that her father's name was "Icadius," not "Icarius"; so it is likely that the problem arose because of a mistake.[20]

In general, the use of the impossible in poetry should be referred to   10
(a) the making of poetry, or to (b) what is better [than what actually exists], or to (c) what is generally accepted.[21] For (a) with respect to the making of poetry, [one may reply that] a plausible impossibility is preferable to an implausible possibility;[22] (b) [as to the impossibility of people being] such as Zeuxis painted them, [one may reply that] it is better to paint them in this manner, for the ideal should be [re-garded as] superior to the real;[23] and (c) as to that which is asserted to

be unreasonable, [one may reply that] this is [what men say] or that
15   there are times when it is not regarded as unreasonable, for even the
improbable has a [mathematical] probability of occurring.[24]

We should consider inconsistencies in poetic expressions in the
same way as we consider refutations in arguments, i.e., we should as-
certain whether by an expression the poet means the same thing, or
the thing in relation to the same thing, or the thing in the same manner, and hence [whether he is inconsistent] with what he himself says
or with what a prudent man would be assumed to say.[25]

20   It is right to censure a poet for using without any necessity what is unreasonable or in bad taste, like the unreasonable appearance of Aegeus
[in the *Medea*] of Euripides or the baseness of Menelaus in the *Orestes*.

Critics, then, advance five kinds of censure; for the poet may use
what is (1) impossible, or (2) unreasonable, or (3) harmful, or (4) inconsistent, or (5) contrary to correctness in accord with art. And the
25   [kinds of] responses to these criticisms must be sought among the
above–mentioned kinds, and there are twelve of these.

26

One might pose the problem whether the epic or the tragic form of
imitation is better. For if the less vulgar [poem] is the better form, and
if such a form is always addressed to the better class of spectators, it is
quite clear that the one which imitates all [kinds of objects] is in bad
taste.[1] [Some performers], thinking that the audience will not per-
30   ceive what is going on unless they add something themselves, indulge
in a great deal of movement [i.e., stage–business], like bad flute–
players who whirl about when they are imitating a discus–throw or
pull at the chorus leader when they are performing the Scylla.[2] Accordingly, for some thinkers tragedy [is thought to be] a form of this
kind, like the new school of performers in the opinion of the old
35   school;[3] thus Mynniscus used to call Callippides "the ape" for his
highly exaggerated manner of performing, and such, too, was the
1462a opinion held about Pindar. [According to these thinkers, then,] the
whole tragic art is to the epic art as the later performers are to the
earlier performers; and they say that the epic art is addressed to
cultivated[4] spectators, who have no need of posturing, whereas the
tragic art is addressed to vulgar spectators. So it is clear, [they con-
clude], that the tragic art, being in bad taste, would be inferior to the
epic art.

(1) The charge, however, applies not to the art of poetry, but to the art of performing, since it is possible even for a rhapsodist to overdo his gestures,[5] which is just what Sosistratus used to do, and so too may a singer in a contest, which is just what Mnasitheus the Opuntian used to do.

(2) Not every kind of movement should be rejected—any more than every kind of dancing—but only the movements of bad performers, which is precisely the censure made of Callippides and of other performers nowadays who imitate [free women] as if they were vulgar.[6]

(3) Tragedy, like epic poetry, produces its effect even without movements of performers, because its quality is evident even from reading it. So if it is superior to epic poetry in all other respects, one may say that at least this [i.e., imitation through movements of performers] is not a necessary attribute of tragedy.[7]

(4) Now, [tragedy excels epic poetry] because it has all [the essential parts] that epic poetry has, and it can even use meter. In addition, no small parts of it are music and spectacle,[8] whereby pleasures are most vividly produced.

(5) Tragedy produces vivid impressions when read as well as when performed.[9]

(6) Tragedy excels epic by achieving the end of imitation in a shorter length of time; for what is more concentrated is more pleasant than what is diluted over a long period of time. For example, what effect would the *Oedipus [Rex]* of Sophocles produce if it were to be stretched into as many epic lines as the *Iliad* has?

(7) Epic imitation has less unity than does tragic, and a sign of this is the fact that more than one tragedy can be made out of one epic. So (a) if only one plot is used by an epic poet, the epic must appear either (i) truncated, if briefly presented, or (ii) diluted, if stretched to the usual length in this meter; but (b) if many [plots are used], that is, if epic consists of many *actions*, [the imitation] will be not a unity but like the *Iliad* and the *Odyssey*, which have many such parts each with a considerable magnitude of its own, although each of these poems is constructed as well as it can be and is, as far as possible, an imitation of a single *action*.[10]

Since, then, tragedy excels epic poetry in all the above [four] respects and also in performing the function proper to the poetic art (for [tragedy and epic] should produce not any chance pleasure but

the one stated earlier), it is evident that, by achieving the function of
15   the poetic art to a higher degree, tragedy is superior to epic poetry.
Concerning tragedy and epic poetry, with respect to each of them
in general, their species and their parts, their number and differences, the *reasons* for their being well or badly constructed, the censures made of them by critics and the responses to those censures, let
the above discussion suffice.

COMMENTARIES ON THE POETICS

The references given in the Commentaries and in the other parts of this work are to the standard pages (sections) and lines according to the Bekker's edition of Aristotle's works (Berlin, 1831). In particular, pages 1447a8–1462b18 cover the treatise on the *Poetics*, and these pages and lines appear as such in the margins of the translation. The Bekker pages covering each of Aristotle's works are as follows.

Categories: 1a1–15b33.
Nature of Propositions (De Interpretatione): 16a1–24b9.
Prior Analytics: 24a10–70b38.
Posterior Analytics: 71a1–100b17.
Topics: 100a18–164b19.
Sophistical Refutations: 164a20–184b8.
Physics: 184a10–267b26.
On the Heavens: 268a1–313b23.
On Generation and Destruction: 314a1–338b19.
Meteorology: 338a20–390b22.
On the Universe, To Alexander: 391a1–401b29.
On the Soul: 402a1–435b25.
On Sensation and Sensibles: 436a1–449a31.
On Memory and Recollection: 449b1–453b11.
On Sleep and Wakefulness: 453b11–458a32.
On Dreams: 458a33–462b11.
On Divination from Dreams: 462b12–464b18.
On Longevity and Shortness of Life: 464b19–467b9.
On Youth, Old Age, Life, and Death: 467b10–470b5.
On Respiration: 470b6–480b30.
On Breath: 481a1–486b4.
On Treatise on Animals: 486a5–638b37.
On Parts of Animals: 639a1–697b30.
On Motion of Animals: 698a1–704b3.

On Locomotion of Animals: 704a4–714b23.
On Generation of Animals: 715a1–789b20.
On Colors: 791a1–799b20.
On Objects of Hearing: 800a1–804b39.
Physiognomy: 805a1–814b9
On Plants: 815a10–830b4.
On Reported Marvels: 830a5–847b10.
Mechanics: 847a11–858b31.
Problems: 859a1–967b27.
On Indivisible Lines: 968a1–972b33.
Positions and Names of Winds: 973a1–b25.
On Xenophanes, Zeno, and Gorgias: 974a1–980b21.
Metaphysics: 980a21–1093b29.
Nicomachean Ethics: 1094a1–1181b23.
Great Ethics: 1181a24–1213b30.
Eudemean Ethics: 1214a1–1249b25.
On Virtues and Vices: 1249a26–1251b37.
Politics: 1252a1–1342b34.
Household Management: 1343a1–1353b27.
Rhetoric: 1354a1–1420b4.
Rhetoric for Alexander: 1420a5–1447b7.
Poetics: 1447a8–1462b18.

COMMENTARIES

1

1. In Aristotle's Theory of Art we have given an adequate account of Aristotle's concept of a science, a productive science, an art, a work of art, the so–called "fine arts" and "useful arts," how these differ from each other and how they are related. We have also shown that poetics, and hence Aristotle's *Poetics*, is a species of a productive science and have discussed the aim of poetics as a species and also as related to man's ultimate good, which is happiness.

As a science, poetics exists primarily in the mind of the poetic scientist but secondarily in books in symbolic form, and it deals exclusively with general or universal concepts and truths about the poetic art (i.e., the art of poetry). The poetic art, on the other hand, can exist as an art only in the mind of the artist; for, whereas a scientist can present his science in symbolic form, an artist, and hence a poetic artist, cannot do this, because art as an ability also requires skill. The artist must not only know the general truths of the corresponding science, which can be presented symbolically, but also have skill and true reason in dealing with individual objects in the production of a work of art, and skill in dealing correctly with individual objects can exist not in vocal or written form but only in the mind of the artist. Moreover, skill as an ability but not in activity can be inferred as existing in the mind but cannot be exhibited.

In general there are three distinct things in matters of art which should not be confused: the science of art, art itself, and the work of art. The science of art (or the productive science) is general knowledge existing primarily in the mind and secondarily in symbolic form; art is a certain ability which can exist only in the mind of the artist, as already stated; the work of art is that which is produced by the artist and which may be either external to the mind, as in the case of a statue, or in the mind, as in the case of a student's knowledge acquired from a teacher who has the art of imparting that knowledge. The work of art is sometimes called "art work" or "artistic work," but often it is called just "art." We shall use consistently the expressions "science of art" (or "productive science"), "art," and "work of art" as we have just specified, unless otherwise indicated; and by "poetry" we shall mean poems collectively. We may add, poems as Aristotle uses the term differ from other works of art by having plots (1447a8–13).

Following the usual translations of Aristotle's *Poetics* into English, we are keeping the term "poem" as the translation of the corresponding Greek term ποίημα (transliterated as "*poiema*"), which had a wide and also a narrow meaning in ancient Greece, although such expressions as "literary composition" and "literary work of art" are perhaps closer in meaning to the Greek term as Aristotle used it in the *Poetics*. The term "*poiema*" in its wide sense signified any fine or useful work of art, but in its narrow sense it signified a poem as Aristotle defined it, i.e., a work of art having a plot. Similarly, the term ποιητική (transliterated as "*poietike*") had two corresponding meanings: its translation in the wide sense is "productive," but in the narrow sense it is "poetic."

2. The species of the poetic art, taken as a genus are: the art of epic, the art of tragedy, the art of comedy, the art of dithyrambs, the art of music, the art of dancing, and, in general, any art which uses a plot. The art of poetry itself is a species of a higher genus, that of the imitative art; this art includes, besides the art of poetry, also the art of painting, the art of making statues, and other imitative arts which do not use plots to produce their works. Evidently, paintings and statues, too, imitate something, but they are static, so to speak, both themselves and with respect to what they imitate. The imitative art itself is a species of a still higher genus, namely, art, which includes also the arts of making useful products, such as houses and machines and the like. Finally, art is a species of ability, and ability is a species of quality, which is an ultimate genus and so a category (9a14–27).

3. Art in general is an ability which the artist has acquired and uses as a moving cause to produce a work of art by bringing into existence the form in a material or materials receptive of that form. For example, the carpenter uses materials, e.g., wood and glue, and with his art transforms them into a table by bringing into existence the form of the table which has been produced. The capacity or effect which an artist has, then, is the ability to bring about or cause in the materials which he or she uses the form of the thing produced, i.e., the form of the work of art.

4. Part (b) in the text shifts from the poetic art to the work of that art and inquires into the manner in which the main part of that work— here, the plot—should be constructed if the work is to be well done.

5. It will be shown later that a tragedy as a work of the corresponding poetic art has qualitative and quantitative parts. Qualitative parts are such as plot, thought, character, and diction (1450a7–10); quantitative parts are such as prologue, episode, and exode (1452b14–27).

6. Such things are, for example, the origin and development of the poetic arts (at least some of them), problems concerning what is correct or incorrect, and the superiority of tragedy over epic. These are treated in Sections 4, 5, 25, 26 of the *Poetics*.

That which is first according to the nature of a thing is the nature and definition of the thing itself, such as the genus or category of the thing, the differentia, and, in general, what Aristotle calls "the causes" of the thing, whether all four causes (form, matter, mover, final cause) or only the ones which the thing has, for not everything has four causes (1417a18–20). The next paragraph of the text mentions imitation as the genus of poetic works of art, and in Section 6, where the discussion of the art of tragedy begins, the full definition of tragedy is given.

For Aristotle, the method of proceeding according to nature amounts to what we call "the scientific method." This method has been discussed to some extent in the Theory of Art. Another method of proceeding is called by Aristotle "that which is clearer to us," and this method usually proceeds for psychological reasons not from the principles of the thing itself but from what we happen to know first about the thing, and such knowledge includes many accidents of the thing which cannot be used scientifically to demonstrate any properties of the thing but which can make it easier for beginners in a subject, especially at the earlier stages of one's learning, to learn the principles of the thing and then demonstrate properties of it (71b33–72a5, 141b3–14, 184a16–b14).

7. Each kind of work of art mentioned here takes some time to be presented in full to the audience, and this seems to indicate that each of them has a plot, as stated in (b) of the first paragraph in the text. One may wonder if the term "plot" is appropriate in a work for the flute or the lyre, but there is movement even in those works with a beginning and a middle and an end, in which case it would appear that a plot exists even in such works, whether univocally or analogously. A symphony, for example, begins with a theme, which is followed by its development, and there is an end; and these three parts differ, as in a tragedy. The same thing would apply to flute–playing and to lyre–playing.

Instead of the term "plot," one might choose another term, such as the term "story" or "tale" or "myth" for the Greek term μῦθος (= "*mythos*"); for the term "*mythos*" had each of these meanings, and many more. The choice of a term, however, is less important than familiarity with different species of what one chooses to translate as "poems," for by perceiving what is common to the various plots in those poems one would be in a better position to perceive by induction and abstraction the meaning of "*mythos*" as Aristotle used the term. As in other translations, we shall use the term "plot."

8. Alternatives to the term "imitation" for the Greek term are "portrayal," "representation," "imaginative description," "idealization," and perhaps others, depending on the poem or the kind of poem. It appears that there is no English term having the wide meaning which Aristotle assigns to the corresponding Greek term. The problem has been discussed in Aristotle's Theory of Art, Part III, and a definition of imitation has been induced from the various places in the *Poetics* where Aristotle uses the term.

9. The means are the material cause or materials which are used to render the imitation, i.e., language, harmony, and rhythm, as Aristotle states later.

10. These are the objects, real or imagined or idealized, which are imitated, e.g., *actions* or feelings.

11. These are the ways in which imitation takes place, e.g., the events may be narrated by one person or represented dramatically by the performers.

What has been said so far about poems is that they are all imitations and differ with respect to the means they use, the objects they imitate, and the manner in which the objects are imitated. It would follow, then, that "imitation" is the genus or a genus of poems.

12. It is evident from this statement that Aristotle regards the arts of painting and of making statues as being imitative, but these arts do not come under the art of poetry, for their corresponding works have no plots but are static imitations, as we have stated. The Greek term translated as "likeness," then, suggests a picture or a statue and the like, and it would appear that "likeness" is a species of "imitation," for "imitation" as a genus is applied also to comedy and tragedy, in which there is *action*.

13. Both art and habit are acquired capacities coming under the category of quality and existing in the mind. Art has been sufficiently

discussed in Aristotle's Theory of Art, Part III. A habit as used in the text here, on the other hand, is (a) a stable quality acquired for the most part by a member or members of a group, (b) usually acceptable to the group, and (c) aimed at the production of works of art usually approved by that group. Thus, artists act by nature or by art in accord with the scientific truths concerning that art in order to produce good works of art, but they act by habit according to what is accepted by a group as good or true and aim to produce what are thought by that group to be good works of art.

14. Should the term here be "voice," which usually appears in English translations, or the term "nature?" In many Greek texts the Greek term which appears is the genitive of φωνή (= "voice"); in other Greek texts the Greek term is the genitive of φύσις (= "nature"). The correct translation should be "nature."

15. Rhythm, language, and harmony are the means or materials which are used to produce works of the poetic art, and there is good reason for them to be stated generically rather than specifically. For, in the production of poetic works of art which is our present concern, i.e., in tragedies, none of the means or materials which may be used should be excluded. Had we, for example, chosen the term "speech" instead of the term "language" among the materials to which meaning is attached, as some translators did, we would have restricted such means to what is spoken or dramatized and would have excluded what is in the form of writing; but a tragedy, being a poem, can be enjoyed according to Aristotle by being read as well as by being dramatized (1450b15–20), and the use of the term "speech" among the means excludes the direct reading of a tragedy, whereas the use of the term "language" includes it. Similarly, the term "harmony" should be so used as to include (a) pleasing musical notes taken singly in succession or simultaneously as in a chord or in some combination of these two, and (b) intonation.

16. If we assume that lyre–playing has a plot, we will have to grant that Panpipe–playing, too, has a plot; and the case for dancing will be even stronger, for we are told that dancing imitates character and feelings and *actions*. Usually, the term "character" refers to the ethical rather than to the intellectual virtues and vices, whereas the term *"thought"* refers to the intellectual vices and virtues.

17. Sophron of Syracuse and his son Xenarchus wrote mimes in

prose, and Socratic dialogues were also written in prose; but these two kinds, although imitations in prose, were not given a name.

18. The translation of the part "*poios*" in the Greek word "*epopoios*" should be not "poet," as some translate it, but "maker" or "producer." The word for "poet" is ποιητής (= "*poietes*").

19. The term "elegiac–maker" means a maker of works of art in elegiac meter, i.e., in couplets in which the first line is dactylic hexameter and the second line is a pentameter comprised of two hemistichs each comprised of two dactyls and a long syllable; and since such works were usually poems, the makers of them were called "poets." Similarly, the term "epic–maker" means a maker of works in epic meter, i.e., in continuous dactylic hexameters.

20. Homer's poems are imitations, which are works of art or productions; Empedocles' works are scientific, which deal with general truths. But an imitation and a statement of truth have nothing in common, nor do a work of art and a science.

21. Greek texts differ as to what Aristotle's exact words were, but from what has been already stated, it is not difficult to interpret his meaning. One might call Chaeremon "a pan–maker," which means a writer who uses all meters. What entitles Chaeremon to be called "a poet," however, is not his use of pan–meters but the fact that his rhapsody is an imitation which has a plot.

22. In the singing of a dithyramb or a nome, language took the form of speech or diction, harmony took the form of song, and rhythm took the form of meter; and all these three means occurred simultaneously. In the Greek performance of a tragedy or comedy, on the other hand, the three kinds of means were not all used simultaneously; choral songs, for example, were used separately.

2

1. The term "those" may refer to the poets who produce the poems, or to the performers, who may or may not be the poets. In the early history of poetry the performers were often the poets themselves.

2. The term "character" here means mainly the ethical virtues or vices or some mixture of these which one has acquired after birth by intention and habituation; so it signifies a certain ethical quality of the agent who is imitated.

3. The expression "men of one kind of character only" signifies not necessarily all the agents in each poem, but usually the protagonist in

each poem. For example, Oedipus in the *Oedipus Rex* of Sophocles is the hero who is above average, but the herdsman is not above average. In comedy, too, not all the agents need be worse than average.

4. Dancing and flute–playing and lyre–playing in this context evidently suggest that Aristotle regards these activities as being imitations with a plot and hence as poetic performances.

5. Is it *"Deiliad"* or *"Deliad?"* Texts differ. If *"Deliad,"* it would mean *The Tale of Delos*, but if *"Deiliad,"* it would mean *The Tale of a Coward* or something of this sort. Perhaps the latter is correct, for the term *"Coward"* suggests a person worse than average or subject to ridicule.

6. The Greek text of this sentence is uncertain, perhaps due to corruption.

3

1. The expression "narrator of a poem" may signify the poet himself or someone else who represents the poet. The same applies to the terms "imitator" and "performer," for each of them may signify the poet or someone who represents the poet.

2. The three primary kinds of activities of man are *actions*, productions, and contemplations. *Actions* are usually ends in themselves and are performed mostly according to ethical habits; contemplations, too, are ends in themselves and are thinking activities, such as the pursuit and possession of truth and of the nature and definitions of things; productions are constructions of objects not as ends in themselves but for the sake of other ends, for houses are built for comfort, and music is produced for man's enjoyment.

3. These are the three differentiae which give rise to different kinds of poems.

4. Sophocles produced tragedies, Homer produced epics, so both produced poems whose main agents are portrayed as being above average. The term "virtuous" here means virtuous above average and not completely virtuous.

5. Sophocles produced tragedies, Aristophanes produced comedies, so both produced poems to be presented dramatically, i.e., to be presented as plays.

6. The Greek terms transliterated as *"dramata"* and *"drondas"* seem to come from the same root.

7. The Dorians were one of the major linguistic and ethnic divisions of the Greeks.

8. The Megarians formed one of the Dorian states, and some of the Peloponnesians who are mentioned later in (2) formed other Dorian states.

9. Epicharmus was a Dorian; he abandoned the use of invectives and employed the ludicrous in comedy.

10. Chionides and Magnes were not Dorians but Athenians, who were another major group of Greeks.

11. The Dorians used the belief that the words "*dran*" and "*dramata*" came from the same root to assert that it was they who had introduced drama in ancient Greece.

4

1. To say here that the two causes are natural is to say that each is a cause existing in a person either (a) as man's nature, or (b) as a part of that nature, or (c) as something which follows man's nature or a part of that nature. Since the causes existing in a person are three (form, matter, and final cause, with one's father, according to Aristotle, being the external moving cause), one should seek the two causes among these three.

2. Imitating is an activity which follows from a part of a person's form, i.e., from a part of his or her soul, but not from the whole form; for there are other kinds of activities which follow from a person's form, e.g., theoretical activity, taking in food, etc., and these are not imitations. Hence imitation, whether as a power or as the activity according to that power, is a cause as a part of a person's form, which is the formal cause or the person's soul, or of the activity of that part.

3. Animals imitate as movers by the use of sensation or imagination; but humans do so by reason as well as by sensation and imagination, for some of their learning which is a form of imitation is acquired from others through reason. Further, the human race has been advancing in the forms of imitation, especially those which require reason, whereas the other animals have shown no such advance at all (according to Aristotle). It is evident, then, that human beings are the most imitative of animals.

4. The enjoyment of imitations, whether one's own or those of others, is the second cause; and it is a part of man's final cause, which is happiness. For what is properly enjoyable contributes to man's happiness, and the enjoyment of works of art has been shown in Aristotle's Theory of Art, Part V, to contribute to man's happiness.

5. Aristotle does not discuss or prove the first of the two causes, for the fact that even infants imitate is an adequate sign of the first cause. But the second cause is less evident and can best be made known by the use of examples which purport to show that, in certain cases, although the perception of certain things is painful, the imitation of them is enjoyable. Aristotle uses an example of this kind. The effect of seeing a real corpse is painful. Since the effect of a work of art which is a good imitation of a real corpse is not painful but pleasurable, it follows that the pleasurable effect must be caused not by the corpse *qua* real, which would be painful, but by the imitation of it. Further, even if the object of imitation were not known, the imitation would still be enjoyable, not *qua* imitating an object, but in virtue of its workmanship, which is skill, and skill is a part of art or of man's nature.

There are two elements, then, which make an imitation enjoyable: the true inference of what the imitation imitates when the object imitated is known, and the workmanship in that imitation. The true inference is like the solution to a problem; and just as such solution is learning and therefore pleasant (1448b13–15), so is the inference of the object imitated from the imitation of that object. As for the accuracy of the workmanship, it arouses wonder and admiration for the artist; and wondering why or how a thing can be or be done in a certain way leads to an inquiry into causes and, on a higher intellectual plane, ultimately to philosophizing.

6. As we stated in Aristotle's Theory of Art, Part III, advance in the arts and in knowledge and progress in general are caused by those who are born with natural gifts and use them.

7. Do the *actions* of noble persons differ from noble *actions*? Usually they do not; but since a tragic end in a tragedy is possible only when an *action* is caused by an error on the part of the protagonist, one or a few of his *actions* will not be noble.

8. Noble *actions* are serious and of great importance, and attending to them rather than to trivial and less important *actions* is the mark of a magnanimous or great person. It would follow, then, that magnanimity belongs to a dignified poet rather than to a less worthy poet, and, in view of this, tragedy would be superior to comedy; for, if A is superior to B, an attribute of A is prior in goodness and hence superior to the corresponding attribute of B (1018b37–8a1).

9. The term "iambic" is derived from the transliterated Greek verb

"*iambizein*," which means to denounce or abuse or lampoon and the like, and since the early Greek poets were lampooning each other in a metrical foot of two syllables, the first unaccented but the second accented or the first short but the second long, they called such metrical verse "*iambos*," which is translated into "iambic."

10. The dramatizing at the early stage of poetry was performed not by a number of performers but by one performer, usually the poet himself, who assumed the role of the various agents in the poem in turn.

11. Aristotle here regards Homer as being the forerunner of both tragedy and comedy.

12. The literal translation of the Greek word is not "tragedians" but "teachers of tragedy." It appears that, in the early years of tragedy, those who taught or directed tragedy were usually the tragedians themselves.

13. From what has already been stated about tragedy, it is not clear whether Aristotle is referring to the four kinds or species of tragedy listed in lines 1455b32–6a3 (the complex tragedy, the tragedy of suffering, the tragedy of character, and the fourth kind whose name does not appear in those lines but appears in lines 1459b8–10) or to something else.

14. To judge tragedy with respect to its nature is to judge it apart from accidental requirements or limitations. In fact, Aristotle's principles of evaluating a tragedy, as enumerated in the *Poetics*, may be used to judge a given tragedy without the need of attending a performance; for, as stated in lines 1450b18–9, the tragic effect or pleasure of a good tragedy may be felt by a sufficiently educated audience even without the use of spectacle.

To judge tragedy in relation to the theater may refer to the limitations which the spectacle may impose on the tragedy or to the kind of audience, or to such other matters as competitions and the like. For example, a weak audience may be unable to appreciate tragic pleasure; hence if the audience fails to be pleased by a good tragedy, the failure will be caused not by the nature of the tragedy but by the weakness of the audience. What would please such audience, then, would be not a good tragedy but one which may add to their contentment but not to their happiness. The difference between happiness and contentment has been discussed in Aristotle's Theory of Art, Part IV.

5

1. 1448a16–18, b34–38.

2. This expression is not a definition of comedy, as some think, but an inductive statement about it. The definition of comedy, like that of tragedy, would differ from that expression.

3. In tragedy, it is a serious error on the part of the protagonist that leads to a tragic event; in comedy, it is a harmless error on the part of the protagonist that leads to a ludicrous event. This comparison leads to a number of analogies, one of which is,

tragic agent : comic agent :: serious error : harmless error.

4. Did Epicharmus and Phormis introduce universality in their plots and language? They did not; for from what follows in the text, it was the Athenian Crates who first used universal language and plots, and Crates lived later. One may say, then, that the three Athenian poets just mentioned, taken together, transformed iambic poetry into comedy as something complete and at its best. Homer, of course, suggested these by abandoning invective and introducing universality and the ludicrous (1448b34–38).

5. This meter is the dactylic hexameter.

6. Commentators differ as to what is meant by "one revolution of the sun." Some take it to state that the performance of a tragedy should last no more than twenty–four hours, others, not more than twelve hours; still others, that the *action* imitated should be represented as taking up no more than twenty–four hours, perhaps this being what is meant. One thing is clear however: the audience should easily perceive the *action* of a good tragedy as a unity and a whole having a beginning, a middle, and an end.

7. There are two kinds of parts, qualitative and quantitative. The parts as qualities of the tragedy are six: plot, character, diction, *thought*, spectacle, and song. Epic poetry has no spectacle or song; the other four parts are common to both epic poetry and tragedy (1450a9–10, 1459b8–11). As for the quantitative parts, they are prologue, episode, exode, and choric song for tragedy (1452b14–27).

6

1. This is epic poetry; it is discussed at greater length in Sections 23 and 24, lines 1459a17–60b5.

2. Most if not all critics have regarded the Greek corresponding to part (4) in our translation of the definition of tragedy, i.e., the phrase "ending through pity and fear in a catharsis of such emotions," as stating the final cause of tragedy in the *Poetics* and, instead of the word "ending" in that phrase, translators have used such words as "achieving," "effecting," and "carrying to completion," which perhaps would be more appropriate if part (4) were to be regarded as the final cause. As a consequence, the difficulty in explaining part (4) as stated by Aristotle gave rise to a wide variety of interpretations, at least some of them hardly convincing. It might appear, however, that the final cause is mentioned earlier in the *Poetics*, and that part (4) might be interpreted not as a final cause but as the manner in which tragedy itself ends. These two points need clarification. First, let us give the somewhat conventional interpretation, along with reasons for it, and then turn to another interpretation, perhaps a new one, which regards the definition of tragedy as including only two causes, the formal and the material.

(A) In the theoretical sciences, which deal with things which exist of necessity or for the most part, a two–part definition consisting of the genus and the differentia is in some cases sufficient. In the productive sciences, which deal with things which may or may not exist, a four–part definition giving the four causes for any species may be preferable. Thus, for example, analysis of the formal, material, and moving causes, once they are stated as the object, means, and manner of tragedy, will yield the six parts in virtue of which a tragedy is of a certain quality.

Now, Aristotle explicitly calls this a definition, and we recognize that it has four parts. If, as is the case, it is a definition of the kind of thing that could have four causes and we identify two or three of those parts as giving causes, then it is probable that the remaining part or parts also give a cause or causes.

Formal. In the definition of tragedy, the first part, drawing on Sections 2 and 5, posits the plot as the formal cause, in which the imitation of a particular kind of *action* is the soul of tragedy.

Material. "Speech with forms of enhancement" means language, rhythm, and harmony, which are given in Section 1 as possible materials for any poetry. Different species of poetry must use one or more of these; tragedy may use all of them as "appropriate to each of its parts."

"A differentia should be subdivided by its own differentia" (1038a). The necessary and sufficient differentiae are rhythm, language, and harmony. Different meters, different diction, or different modes of music are not essential differences, though one or the other of these may be more "appropriate"; the change from trochaic tetrameter to iambic trimeter (1449a20), for example, was not a change from one poetic species to another but a change from less good to better tragedy in the historical evolution of that species.

Moving (or *Efficient*). The moving cause is expressed in "presented in a dramatic and not a narrative manner." A poet, or his poetic art, produces a poem. Specifically, a narrator, or his art of narration, produces a narrative, e.g., an epic; a dramaturge, i.e., a poet producing in the dramatic manner, or his art of dramaturgy, produces a drama, e.g., a comedy or a tragedy.

The performers are accidental causes, whereas the dramaturge is the essential cause. The tragedy exists without performers but not without the dramaturge. Different performers may perform the same tragedy. The performers, then, are the moving cause of this or that performance but not of the tragedy; consequently, one may have a bad performance of a good tragedy.

Final. We do not deliberate about ends but only about means. Thus, there is no demonstration of any kind in the *Poetics* about the final cause of poetry.

Aristotle asserts repeatedly that "the [tragic] poet should produce through imitation the kind of pleasure that comes from pity and fear (1453b10)." That is what he *must* aim at if he is to produce a tragedy. The *Poetics* deals mostly with the ways in which he can achieve that end. The ways are subject to deliberation and choice between better and worse.

Pleasure is an effect of all imitation, though the proximate final cause may be something else; e.g., one may imitate to teach or learn. The essential final cause of poetic imitation, however, is uniquely pleasure. Of course, poems may be used for other ends, e.g., to teach or to make money, but that is outside of the art of poetry.

The emotions of tragic pity and fear are not those caused by actual conditions of an individual's everyday life. Just as the cause of the tragic emotions is an imitation, so those emotions are in some sense imitative. The spectator comes to the tragic theater expecting to undergo a kind of pity and fear but with the understanding that the "causes" will leave with the exodus, if not before; they will not be at home waiting for him.

By nature, the spectator shares to some degree in the natural gift of the poet who can mold himself to any emotion. The particular necessities and probabilities which determine the fortunes of the protagonist, i.e., of one like himself, are not the spectator's. Insofar as they are general, he can view them as potential for himself, but he can deny their actuality for himself. Thus, whatever the exact meaning of "catharsis," it may reflect Plato's theory of the impure pleasures; i.e., pity and fear are painful and the pleasure follows from the relief of that pain.

The thinker meditating on the "moral lesson" of a tragedy may experience the pure pleasure of contemplation, but that is not the pleasure proper to poetry.

Let us now turn to the other interpretation.

(B) It is stated in lines 1448b5–19 that all men enjoy imitations in general, and more so if these are accurately produced; and they enjoy them because they are pleased by learning through them. So it would follow that tragedies, being imitations, would be enjoyable. Now Aristotle's first concern in the *Poetics* is the art of producing, not any kinds of tragedies, but good tragedies, and usually these can be enjoyed not by the common people, but by mature spectators with good taste, as implied by lines 1453a33–36, b8–11, and elsewhere; and such spectators are likely to be the citizens of a good rather than of a bad state. It appears, then, that such citizens go to see a good tragedy not to get rid of their personal troubles or emotional excesses, but for the sake of enjoyment; and this is also evident from the facts themselves and by induction. One should include in that enjoyment a sense of wonder and an understanding of why and how an error in judgment or lack of knowledge can cause an eminent person to suffer undeserved misfortune under certain circumstances. One might also add the following: the spectator's admiration for the poet who conceived by his or her art or natural gift the initial conditions that led by their nature to a tragic or almost tragic end, an experience of the right kind of pity (as defined by Aristotle) that one should have for persons of a certain kind who suffer undeserved misfortune, the enhancements of the performance, and perhaps others; but some of these may not be necessary parts of the enjoyment or of the final cause.

As for the part (4) in the translation of the definition of tragedy, perhaps its function for the spectator may be understood if the consequences of its omission from the tragedy are considered; for the spectator's feelings for the hero and his understanding of the tragedy's outcome would then be left unresolved, hanging, incomplete, without purpose or what one might call "the moral of the tragedy" or, to use the language of the text, without a catharsis of the spectator's feelings for the hero, without a realistic understanding of the natural causes and effects in certain human affairs or events, and perhaps without one's proper attitude when faced with similar situations.

But, one might assert, the definition of tragedy as given here should include all four causes, yet it appears that it does not. First, the moving cause is not included in the definition; for the cause of a tragedy's existence is the poet or the art of the poet who produced it, and this is discussed in general at length in the *Metaphysics* (1032a12–34b19). One might also assert that the performers are the moving cause, and these are mentioned by the word "*drondon*" in the definition. But the performers might be held to be the moving cause of the *performance* of the tragedy and not of the tragedy itself as a whole, for the tragedy will still exist and be read even without being performed.

On the other hand, the moving cause has already been mentioned in the first sentence of Section 4 by the phrase "imitating is innate in men," where "imitating," when actualized, includes, among other things, "producing tragedies" as one of its species. The final cause, too, is mentioned in Section 4. In fact, the two causes in Section 4 are, in the order mentioned, the moving cause and the final cause, the moving cause being imitating, for it is the tragic poet who does the imitating by producing a tragedy, and the final cause being the pleasure from learning and the enjoyment by seeing a tragedy.

It remains to show that the definition given of tragedy here includes only the formal cause and the material cause. The two parts of the formal cause are the genus and the differentia or differentiae. The genus is "an imitation" and appears in (1) of the definition, and the rest of (1) states partly the object of imitation or the plot, or else it specifies the kind of imitation as a lower genus, if you wish; (2) states the means used in that imitation; (3) states the manner of imitation; and (4) states the plot's ending, which is a part of the object of imitation, specifically a necessary aspect of the construction since the concept of the *ending* of a plot implies not only formal closure but its effect, the dissipation of the audience's attention and involvement. We have, then, the genus and the three differentiae in the definition, and these are mentioned also in Section 1. But where do we find the material cause? If we regard (2) as stating the material cause, we neglect the means as one of the differentiae. Does (2), then, include both the material cause and the three differentiae? The problem concerns the nature of definition, and it belongs to the *Metaphysics*. We need not go into the details for the metaphysical solution, but a simple example may suggest the solution.

Rhythm is one of the means used by certain poems, and it is possible for two poems to differ by using different rhythm; for the hexameter is the proper rhythm for epic but the trimeter is the proper rhythm for iambic. So both epic and iambic use rhythm as a material cause. But epic differs from iambic with respect to rhythm, and the difference is caused by using different kinds of meter or rhythm. Thus, even if both poems have rhythm, what causes them to be different with respect to rhythm is the two different specifications of rhythm. It is evident, then, that rhythm *qua* rhythm, which is a genus or matter (1024b6–9, 1038a5–9, 1057b37–8a2, 21–25), is present in both epic and iambic as a material cause, but if specified as hexameter in one poem and as trimeter in the other poem, it causes distinct differentiae in the two poems. So (2) in the definition of tragedy performs two functions, that of material cause in one respect, and that of differentia in another respect (1024b6–9). The same applies to harmony and language.

The definition of tragedy, as we have stated it, appears to have four parts, each of which seems to give one of the four causes of tragedy. Such sectioning of the definition, however, did not appear in the original Greek, for punctuation did not exist at that time; it has been introduced by interpreters for the sake of the reader. We may add, it may be so sectioned as to reveal only the formal and the material causes. This will be done in a more complete work on Aristotle's *Poetics*.

Since poems imitate character as well as *action* and feeling according to lines 1447a27–28, one would expect the definition of tragedy to include "character" also. Besides, character is discussed at length in Section 15, and the function of a good tragedy cannot be achieved well without character of a certain kind (1452b28–3a39). On the other hand, *actions* are impossible without character and *thought* and hence are defined partly in terms of these, for a definition of a thing must state the causes. So "character" is implied or included in the definition of *action* and hence of tragedy as it is defined. Further, since serious and important *actions* in tragedies are attributed to persons above average, this fact, too, indicates that the protagonist must be of a certain kind of character, i.e., an agent above average, if his or her fall is to cause fear and pity.

Perhaps the reason why Aristotle mentions character at the start of the *Poetics* in line 1447a28, we may add, is the fact that he has not yet shown that *action* necessitates character, and a reader who is not familiar with Aristotle's methodology will be informed later that character and *thought* are included. The definition of tragedy, however, should not mention explicitly character or *thought*, for these are included in the definition of *action*, otherwise there will be a duplication, which should be avoided in a definition.

If, according to lines 1450b18–19, a good tragedy can produce its effect even without being dramatized by performers, it would seem that the term "language" rather than the term "speech" should be the translation of the Greek term "*logos*"; for one may read a tragedy, and "language" includes "reading." Lines 1449b31–34, however, state that spectacle and singing are necessary parts of tragedy. Besides, every part of a definition is necessary in its application if the essence of a thing as defined is to be specifically represented in that definition (1043b34–44a1). The term "*logos*," then, should be translated as "speech," if the dramatic presentation of a tragedy by performers is to have its full effect.

3. Perhaps this sentence in the manuscript is textually corrupt. An alternative to "intonation or song" is "harmony or meter."

4. The *action* meant is not that of the poet or the performer but that of the agents who are imitated.

5. *Thought* and character as used here are qualities and not activities. One may have a *thought* without *thinking*, as in sleep. To use an analogy, *thought* is to *thinking* as vision is to seeing.

6. Character includes only or primarily one's ethical habits, whether these be virtues or vices or a combination of both. *Thought* includes the ideas of the intellect, those of production, and the ethical or practical ideas; but in the formation and use of character, most of the *thinking* is ethical or practical, for *thinking* in mathematics or

physics or in general in the theoretical sciences is concerned mainly with what is true of necessity or for the most part but does not affect character, whereas ethical or practical *thinking* is concerned with a part of what may or may not be, and it is mostly with the aid of such *thinking* that character is acquired and used.

7. Arguing is drawing conclusions, whether syllogistically or inductively or dialectically or rhetorically or sophistically or in some other way. A *judgment* in the primary sense is a right or true universal belief of a fair–minded man concerning particulars which may or may not exist or come to be (1143a19–24), e.g., "all the world's a stage"; in a secondary sense, however, it is a belief which appears to be a *judgment* in the primary sense, and it may be universal or about a particular.

8. These are the qualitative parts of tragedy; they characterize a tragedy as being of a certain quality or kind. The quantitative parts of a tragedy are considered in Section 12.

9. The means are diction and song; the manner is the spectacle, for tragedy as defined is dramatized by performers on the stage and not narrated; the objects imitated are character, *thought*, and plot or *action*.

10. Since *actions* (in the primary sense) can exist only in humans and not by themselves, one may be inclined to assert that tragedy is an imitation of persons, who are the subjects; but such a stand is indefinite and not specific. One may be imitated in various ways, that is, with respect to each of a variety of attributes or parts, e.g., with respect to appearance, or with respect to movements, or with respect to speech, and so on. By saying that tragedy is an imitation of *action*, one limits that imitation to *actions* of persons.

11. Virtues are habits or qualities acquired not for their own sake but for the sake of the corresponding activities, for happiness exists in certain activities, e.g., in *actions* and not in virtues, which as such are stable qualities but may be dormant.

12. It is not difficult to show that, of the six qualitative parts of tragedy listed earlier, the plot as a complete *action* is the most important part and the end, not *of* tragedy as a whole, but as a part *in* tragedy, for it is the form of tragedy. Spectacle, although an enhancement, is hardly a part coming under the poetic art and may even be omitted without lessening appreciably the effect of a good tragedy (1450b18–19); still, its presence enlivens the plot, and it is used for the sake of the plot. The character of the protagonist and of the other agents, too, is for the sake of the plot, which is the whole *action*, and

knowledge of their character helps the audience understand why the agents perform the kind of *actions* which they choose; and similar remarks apply to *thought*. Diction, too, is instrumental to the plot; for its presence accentuates and embellishes the effect of character and *thought* and *action* and so contributes to a vivid and believable presentation of the plot. It is evident, then, that the plot is the end and the most important part in tragedy and that the other parts are instrumental to that end.

13. By definition, tragedy is an imitation of a serious *action*; hence without that *action*, which is the form in tragedy, there can be no tragedy, just as without a soul there can be no human being or any living thing.

14. The phrase "tragedy would exist without character" means, as indicated in this sentence, not that the agent has no character at all; one's character is hardly brought out by the poet in the tragedy, whether through speech or *action* or in some other way, but it is weakly suggested or implied. That such tragedies are produced by young more than by older poets is to be expected. Revealing character adequately or well requires much knowledge of human nature and hence much experience; so, other things being equal, older poets have an advantage over young poets in attending to character and showing with probability its effect on *actions*. Further, since *actions* are caused by character and *thought*, if character is absent or deficiently treated in tragedy, the causes of events in the plot will be less apparent and hence less persuasive or convincing.

15. Reversals and recognitions are discussed in Section 11.

16. Since *action* or the plot is the most important qualitative part and the end in tragedy, whereas the other five qualitative parts have been shown to be instrumental and as if they were, in a way, the material cause of that end, it is evident that poor materials but a good end make a better tragedy than good materials but a poor end. Hence more emphasis should be placed on plot than on character or diction or *thought*. One may say, then, that, in a way, the plot is to the other five parts of tragedy as form is to matter; for, in a way, means are to ends as matter is to form.

17. This metaphor may be analyzed as follows. In tragedy, the whole *action* or the plot is to the other qualitative parts as form is to matter; for those parts, being instrumental to the plot, are in a way related to it as matter is related to form. Similarly, the body is to the soul in a person as matter is to form. So since the soul of a person, being

noble and honorable according to line 402a1, is the first principle and hence the most important part of that person (415b9–14), such choice makes the metaphor impressive.

18. The whole *action* or the plot is the activity of the agents according to their character, i.e., according to their ethical or practical habits; for *action* requires character and includes it in its definition. Thus character is necessary and instrumental to *action*, and as such it is in a way related to *action* as matter is related to form, or, as it is said in lines 412a19–24, as the first actuality to the second actuality of the soul, or, as inactivity to activity.

None of the other four qualitative parts is as closely related to *action* as is character. For, spectacle and song may even be omitted without lessening appreciably the effect of a good tragedy, as already stated, and so they rank last (1450b18–19). Diction and *thought*, however, are necessary in the plot, but they are not related to plot or *action* as closely as is character. *Thought*, however, should precede diction; for *thought* comes under the objects imitated whereas diction comes under the means of imitation (1450a7–12), and the means are used for the sake of the objects which are imitated.

19. The finest colors laid down without order are good materials without form or with chaotic form; a sketch in black and white, on the other hand, is a composite of poor materials but with a definite form and so imitates something. Evidently, a composite with poor materials but with a definite form is better than a multitude of the finest materials without form or with chaotic form, as stated earlier. The expression "without order" does not mean that there is no order at all; it means that there is disorder or a chaotic order, which is the contrary and not the contradictory of order (11a15–14a25), and in such order there is no imitation.

20. The expression "what there is to be said" refers to facts, opinions, arguments, etc., posited by the poet in the tragedy as held by the agents; the expression "what is fitting" refers to making the most of what there is to be said, i.e., stating the right things in the right manner to the right person at the right time for the right purpose, etc., if these are to have the desired effect in the tragedy, whether with respect to revealing character or *thought* or persuading others by means of argument.

21. Intention is a decision reached after deliberation and is concerned with pursuing or avoiding *actions* and other practical matters

and ends. But such deliberation requires ethical habits, whether virtues or vices; and speech which makes such intentions known reveals ethical habits or character.

22. 1449b34–35.

23. One may express meanings in various ways, e.g., by the use of metaphors, similes, foreign terms, intonation, meters and their composition, etc.

7

1. 1449b24.

2. It is a mistake to say, as some do, that a whole having no magnitude has the same meaning as a whole which is very small, for there are wholes which have no magnitude at all. For example, the human soul has distinguishable parts, i.e., the nutritive, the sentient, the thinking, and the other parts. But although a person as a composite has magnitude and is divisible as a magnitude, no soul, which is a form, has magnitude; for if it had magnitude, since it is only a body that has magnitude, two magnitudes would occupy the same space, and this is impossible. Nor is the soul a whole number; for it is neither odd nor even nor a multitude of units. The soul does have parts, but its parts are not units; for units are not distinguishable, but the parts of the human soul are distinct. One soul may have more distinguishable parts than another, but neither of the two souls is a quantity; both are forms of material substances (204a8–13, 1078a23–24).

3. The kind of beginning meant by Aristotle here is that which is a part of a whole. So although it may follow in time another thing, it does so not of necessity nor as a part of another whole but is the beginning of a whole. The use of the expression "by its nature comes after another" indicates that that which comes after another does so of necessity or for the most part. So the sequence "the beginning, the middle, and the end" constitutes a whole whose parts form a unity by virtue of necessity or high probability. For example, the planting of seed need not take place; but if it does, it is a beginning followed by growth and ending in a tree. Games, too, are wholes in this sense.

4. 1078a36–b2.

5. A tragedy should be judged according to the degree it has succeeded in fulfilling the artistic requirements of good tragedy. Dramatic competitions may impose such restrictions on the quality of a tragedy as (1) fixing the time limits of performances, thus disturbing

the quality of the tragedy by compelling the poet or performers to increase or diminish the natural time or length of the tragedy, or (2) using poor judges, or (3) catering to the wishes of the audience, and perhaps others.

6. To grasp a plot as a whole is to grasp the main parts (i.e., its beginning, middle, and end) and their unity at the same time (1459b18–20).

7. It is such a sequence which causes the unity or form of the plot or tragedy. If the sequence of the events is not such as stated, there is no unity, for those events, not being probable or necessary, will be a chance multitude without form.

8. It is an error to translate the Greek term "*eutychia*," as "happiness," as some do; it should be translated as "good fortune." Happiness is attained not by good fortune, which is a cause external to a person, but under normal conditions with the aid of virtue, which must be acquired by that person.

8

1. The full meaning of the phrase "because of his art or his nature" has been discussed at length in Part III of Aristotle's Theory of Art.

2. The two events are distinct, for the later of the two events did not follow from the earlier, whether of necessity or with high probability. Although it falls outside the plot, the wounding of Odysseus is relevant in the plot (*Od.* 19, 392–466) and so is a part of a single event and of the whole *action*; the feigning of madness, on the other hand, is not relevant as a single event in the *Odyssey* and should not appear. Whether the two events mentioned appeared in a lost work or not is not known; but if they did appear, each would have had to be a contributory part of a single event or *action* in the plot, just as the wound is when the maid recognizes Odysseus.

3. The unity of the whole *action* referred to appears in lines 1450b23–27, and the unity of the *Odyssey* is stated in Section 17, lines 1455b17–23.

4. To take an example, the parts of the word "heat" are its letters as elements. But if the letter "e" is transposed to the end of the word, the meaning of the word "hate," which is formed, differs from the meaning of the word "heat." Isomers in chemistry are another such example. Again, a pound of weight gained or lost is not a part of a man's nature, for that nature as a unity or a whole is not changed by that gain or loss.

9

1. The Greek term εἰκός (= "*eikos*") is usually translated as "probable" in the *Poetics*; it means that which is expected or likely to happen or that which happens or would happen most of the time; we shall translate it in the same way. This kind of probability should not be confused with mathematical probability, which ranges from 0 to 1 but applies to any event which is possible, whether it happens most of the time or by accident or of necessity or never, for some things which are possible may never happen.

2. Since the agents in tragedy, and in drama in general, stand for types of men and not for actual individuals, any chance names may be attached to them for the sake of distinguishing them as types. Sometimes the name chosen suggests the agent's character to which it is attached, as in the case of "Mrs. Malaprop" in Sheridan's *The Rivals*, and "Thrasymachus" in Plato's *Republic*.

3. The pronoun "we" does not include Aristotle himself; it is used idiomatically for men of a certain kind; the word "somehow" which follows tends to confirm this.

4. Those who are so disposed, however, are not right or not necessarily right, for they are persuaded by the evidence of what actually happened and have not yet matured enough to think logically and scientifically about the mathematical probability of what is possible.

5. The phrase "made up" may mean any chance names which do not stand for actual individuals, or else newly coined names; it makes no difference, for both kinds of names signify types and not actual individuals. See also Comm. 2 of this Section.

6. The reference is to lines 1451a38–b5.

7. Specifically stated, a sequence of events which actually happen has a small *mathematical probability* of being necessary or probable. This means that, of the great number of past sequences, there are very few which are necessary or probable, and these would be suitable material for tragedies.

8. Perhaps there is some corruption in the Greek text. If the Greek term ἁπλῶν (= "of simple," in the plural) is kept, the resulting translation, which is "Of simple plots and *actions* the episodic are the worst," leaves out plots and *actions* which are not simple. Bywater sees the difficulty and has the right idea of what Aristotle means; but he seems to use an artificial explanation to justify the text as given. Butcher,

too, grasps Aristotle's meaning; he thinks that the Greek term should be ἄλλων (= "of the others," in the plural), but he does not translate according to that emendation. Also Lucas perceives Aristotle's meaning, but in saying that the Greek term is used technically and is explained in line 1452a12, he errs; for the term is never so used.

Our explanation is simple. If the last letter of the Greek term is changed to "s", the term becomes ἁπλῶς (= "without qualification"); then the resulting translation becomes "Without qualification, plots and *actions* which are episodic are the worst," which is another way of saying that plots and *actions* which are episodic are without exception the worst.

9. If the episodes do not follow each other according to probability or necessity, there is no unity but, if at all, a number of unrelated episodes which do not constitute a unified tragedy.

10. The terms *"chance"* and "luck" are not used synonymously here, as some translators think. *Chance* and luck differ, but both are moving causes and move accidentally. *Chance* is a mover but is inanimate; luck is a mover operating by means of deliberation or *thought* or design.

Aristotle's point here is that, since events which follow each other of necessity or with probability have greater unity, are more persuasive and believable as real, and have greater effect on audiences than events which follow from chance causes, the poet should so choose and structure the events of the plot that accidental or chance causes are kept to a minimum.

10

1. To have unity, an *action* must be complete and a whole, i.e., it must have a beginning and a middle and an end, no essential part should be missing, superfluous things should not be included, the events should follow according to probability or necessity, and the sketch of the plot should be easily grasped and held in memory.

2. The changes meant are in both simple and in complex plots; the latter include reversals and recognitions, which are defined in the next Section.

3. Events which come after or follow previous events may or may not be caused by those events. If they are caused, they follow of necessity or with probability; if they are not caused, they follow by accident. Events in temporal sequence, then, do not necessarily imply

that events which follow are caused by events which immediately precede them.

11

1. 1450a33–35, 1452a16–20.

2. The two contrary events in the example are: coming to cheer Oedipus and making Oedipus eventually miserable, the first being an intended event but the second being an actual event. The event concerning Lynceus which follows has in a sense a double contrariety, one about Lynceus and the other about Danaus; but what made this possible is not stated here.

3. In *Oedipus Rex*, Oedipus becomes miserable immediately upon learning who he is.

4. Perhaps the reference is to the phrase "through an inanimate or animate cause." Recognition through an inanimate object would be, for example, through a necklace (1454b24–5), but through an animate object it would be, for example, through the wound of Odysseus, as in the Bath Scene, or through memory, as in lines 1454b37–5a2. Both are recognitions by chance; the first by *chance* or an inanimate object, the second by luck or an animate object.

5. 1449b24–28.

12

1. 1449b21–50a12.

2. The term "prologue" needs no explanation. An episode is one whole part of the plot and corresponds to one act or scene of a modern play. An exode is a song of the chorus sung as it departs at the end of the performance. A parode is a choral song sung during the entrance of the chorus and follows immediately the prologue. A stasimon is a choral song sung between two successive episodes after the chorus has taken its place at the altar or orchestra.

3. These are sung by one or more performers and differ from those sung by the chorus alone.

4. These are lamentations sung by the chorus together with one or more performers.

13

1. The reference is to Sections 6 to 12.

2. Aristotle will now discuss the properties of tragedy which will achieve its function.

3. As described in Section 10, a complex tragedy is one which includes reversal or recognition or both as elements or parts, and these add surprise and enhance the tragic function.

4. Fair–minded *men* are *men* of great virtue, especially the virtue which is directed towards others and is called "equity" or "fair–mindedness." This virtue is superior to legal justice and requires understanding and prudence. The *actions* of such *men* are not likely to lead to tragedy. If terrible things befall them, as in the case of Socrates, they are external and not caused by errors in judgment, and they are repugnant or repellent or shocking but not pitiful or fearful.

5. We have no compassion for a wicked *man* who changes from misfortune to good fortune, nor do we fear for or pity him.

6. An utterly worthless *man* has very little intellect and is defective in ethical virtues; he is like a slave or a moron and neither fair–minded nor wicked. If he suffers terrible things, we may feel sorry for the poor fellow, but we do not fear for him, for he is not like us, nor do we pity him, for he is likely to suffer because he does not know better.

7. An alternative to "not differing [from us]" is "not excelling us by much," for the Greek name had these two meanings.

8. Perhaps the term "virtue" here includes only the ethical virtues, if by "justice" Aristotle means "fair–mindedness," which is justice in the primary sense and is better than legal justice.

9. A *man* of reputation would value rank and honor and friendship and other such things more than would a *man* who pursues philosophy or any theoretical pursuit, and he would be affected by their loss more than would a *man* who pursues theoretical activities. So, being a *man* of *action*, he would be one to be pitied for such loss more than would a scientist or a philosopher.

10. Can an error be a flaw or a fault or some other such vice, however small? Aristotle's statements do not appear to support this view. In fact, lines 1453a7–10 exclude wickedness, which causes unjust *actions* towards others, and also vice, which may be any of the other bad ethical habits.

The same conclusion appears to follow from the following argument. The same misfortune is more undeserved when caused by an error in judgment than when caused by vice; for, when caused by an error in judgment, which is not a habit, it is less blameworthy than when caused by vice (1105a28–33), which is acquired by prior choice or intention. Further, misfortune is more pitiful when it is less blameworthy than when it is more blameworthy. Hence, since the better tragedy is the one in which the cause makes the protagonist more pitiful, that cause would be an error in judgment and not a vice.

Now Aristotle speaks not of the best tragedy but of the finest tragedy, in which the protagonist should be neither fair–minded, nor wicked, nor yet utterly worthless, as stated in (1), (2) and (3) in Section 13 of the text. The extreme case will then arise if the misfortune occurs by accident, when the protagonist is in no way a cause. In that case, the events occur not of necessity nor with probability but by accident, nor do we have any reversal or recognition or catharsis; in fact, we have no tragedy as a poem, but something repugnant. So the misfortune meant must be caused somehow by the *action* of the protagonist; and that *action*, if it is to arouse fear and pity the most, should be unintentional and not premeditated or not done with full knowledge of the particulars which caused it (1105a28–33).

But a problem appears to arise. Aristotle speaks of the finest tragedy according to art, and one may wonder whether by "the finest tragedy" he means a single tragedy or a tragedy of one kind. If a single tragedy, the events in it must proceed according to necessity or probability, each of these events will have to be unique, and all of them taken together and functioning like premises will lead to a single conclusion or outcome, and all other tragedies will have to be inferior. If so, the tragedy will hardly differ from a demonstration, which is a scientific process and a part of a science. But we are in the field of art and not of science.

The above difficulty may be avoided if the nature of an unintentional *action* is closely examined. Such an *action*, if caused by, say, an error in judgment, may take on many forms, in fact, an indefinite number of them. The victim may be a mother or a son or a friend, etc., and he or she may be killed or delivered to the enemy or deprived of the means to happiness, etc. Further, corresponding to each kind of *action* by the protagonist, the poet may choose characters in an indefinite number of ways and in an indefinite number of settings, as long as each choice is made according to all the principles of the tragic art.

It is evident, then, that there can be an indefinite number of finest tragedies. What makes them finest is that they are all of one kind, that is, they all conform to all the principles of the tragic art. It also follows that both freedom and necessity (or determinism, if you wish) must enter as principles in the construction of a tragedy which is to be of the finest kind. The poet is free to choose characters and settings and *actions* and the like in an indefinite number of ways. Those choices, however, are not capricious, for they should be so limited as to be in accord with the definition and the principles and theorems of the tragic science. Such choices, of course, are relatively very few as compared to capricious choices; and since they are beginnings of tragedies and not principles of any science, they depend entirely on the artists, that is, on their ability to think them out and construct them.

11. It is evident from what follows in this Section that, in the finest tragedies, the expression "single plot" excludes change from misfortune to good fortune. The *Oedipus* is an example. Further, a change from good fortune to misfortune should require also reversal and recognition according to lines 1450a33–35.

12. Perhaps by "grave error" Aristotle means one whose consequences lead to great misfortune.

13. Such a *man* was said to be of average virtue and like us, if we are to be affected by pity and fear for him (1453a5–6). Now we are told that such a *man* may be better rather than worse than we are. If he is better, still he should be not so much better that we no longer fear for him or pity him but better only to such a degree that he is more like us than unlike us. In this way, his fall would be more tragic than if he were exactly like us, for a grave error by a *man* somewhat more virtuous than we are tends to make us aware that it would lead to greater misfortune than does an error by a *man* like us.

14. Perhaps this condition is added because the art of performing what is the finest or the best is better and more difficult than the art of performing what is less than the finest or the best, respectively. So since the most tragic poem is better and more difficult to produce and perform than is a poem which is less tragic, and since performance of a poem is to the poem performed as an attribute is to a subject, it is evident that the performance of a most tragic poem is more difficult than the performance of a poem which is less tragic (993a30–b7, 1018b37–19a1).

15. 1453b27–29, 1454a37–b2, b28–34, 1456a25–28, 1461b19–21.

16. The double construction of the *Odyssey* includes the change for

Odysseus from misfortune (Poseidon has barred his way home) to good fortune (he returns home) and the change for the suitors from good fortune (they are squandering Odysseus' wealth) to misfortune (they are slain by Odysseus).

17. The more the spectators tend to be the common people, the less they are inclined to appreciate tragic pleasure, for their taste for such pleasure is rather weak. Evidently, poets who are victors in a people's rule—i.e., mob rule—would be losers in an aristocracy, if victory depends on applause by the audience or on inferior judges.

18. The term "tragic pleasure" here means the kind of pleasure which a spectator with good taste will get by viewing a tragedy of the finest kind. 1453b9–11.

19. Nothing is known of such a play, if it was written, but Aristotle's point is clear.

14

1. From spectacle as such we receive sensations and appearances, which as such do not reveal the causes of events but at best exemplify or suggest those causes. The composition of events, on the other hand, even if gathered by reading or spoken by others, states the *thought* universally and is therefore more philosophical than is spectacle as such.

2. Literally, the translation of the Greek word is "prior," which has many senses. In this context, "prior" means prior in goodness or in final cause, and the term "better" or "superior" may be used (14a26–b8, 1018b9–19a14). It follows from the preceding Commentary that a poet who attends to the construction of the events more than to spectacle is better than the poet who attends to spectacle more than to the construction of events.

3. Is the term "shudder" synonymous with the term "fear," as some translators think? A person's fear as such is not necessarily visible to others. Perhaps "shudder" signifies strong fear accompanied by trembling or some other such visible sign.

4. The art of presenting a good tragedy on stage is stagecraft and not a part of the art of constructing a good tragedy. If a tragedy is well constructed, stagecraft may enliven that tragedy but cannot change its essence. Bad stagecraft, on the other hand, may even distort that essence by presenting it with monstrous excesses.

5. Such *action* may arouse compassion or fellow–feeling for the vic-

tim, but not pity (as defined by Aristotle) for the agent; for the victim is an enemy, or neither an enemy nor one dear to the agent.

6. The victim, if a relative or a friend of the agent, should be treated well by the agent. If, unknowingly or unintentionally, the agent treats the victim badly, the agent will suffer for that *action* after recognizing the victim later and hence deserves pity. For example, the protagonist in *Oedipus Rex* unwittingly curses himself and condemns himself to exile.

7. To disturb a traditional plot is to change the main or central facts of the story, such as the fact that Clytaemnestra was killed by her son Orestes. To devise incidents is to introduce *actions* or facts or events in general not mentioned in the story, and what is introduced should be in accord with necessity or probability of events and with the other principles of the poetic art. For example, in the *Odyssey* Agamemnon is murdered by his rival and enemy, Aegisthus. To make the story more tragic, Aeschylus, in his *Agamemnon*, has Clytaemnestra, Agamemnon's wife, do the deed; and he makes that more probable by introducing such episodes as the watchman on the roof, the home-coming reception, and the appearance of Cassandra.

8. *Medea*, by Euripides. 1236.

9. Telegonus, the son of Odysseus by Circe, sent by Circe in search of his father, is mistaken by him for a marauder. In the fight that ensues, Telegonus wounds Odysseus fatally before discovering who he is.

10. Are the terms "finest" as used in Section 13 and "best" as used here synonyms? If so, we will have a contradiction with what follows. But see Comm. 15 of this Section.

11. Merope thought that her son was an enemy (1111a11–12).

12. 1455b2–12.

13. Nothing is known about this tragedy.

14. 1453a16–22. See also Comm. 16 of this Section.

15. A tragedy that is to be of the best kind must have a plot which is well organized according to the principles of the tragic art. We have shown in Comm. 10 of Section 13 that, according to the tragic art, there can be an indefinite number of finest tragedies, each of which changes from good fortune to misfortune and includes recognition or reversal or both. Now the terms "finest" and "best" as Aristotle uses them are not synonyms, contrary to the way some translate the corresponding Greek terms. Evidence of this is the fact that both the third and the fourth possibilities considered in lines 1453a17–23, i.e., those of *acting* or of being about to *act*, but not knowingly, come

under the finest tragedies according to the tragic art, but the fourth is regarded as the best, whereas the third is regarded as the next best (1454a2–9). In other words, "the finest kind of tragedy" acts like a genus of the third and the fourth possibilities, for both of these two include pity and fear, yet Aristotle chooses the fourth as the best. Perhaps Bywater gives the right *reason* for this choice; for he says that, unlike the third possibility, the fourth does not offend our moral sensibility. What he means is that the shock or emotion which the spectators would feel if the tragic deed were to be realized would carry some element of repugnance, but that element is avoided in the fourth possibility.

16. We are told in Section 13 that the requirements for tragedies of the finest kind are such that, within families or among friends, historic events which can serve as material for such tragedies are very few. Accordingly, this fact is given in line 1454a9 as the *reason* why the best tragedies which use historical material for construction are also few, as a matter of fact, even fewer than the finest tragedies. For, it was shown that tragedies of the best kind are also of the finest kind but that not all tragedies of the finest kind are of the best kind.

The same conclusion, we may add, can be shown to follow from premises which involve art, luck, and one's nature. In short, highly organized events of a certain kind, like the tragedy of the best kind, do actually happen but do so very infrequently, for there is a very small mathematical probability for them. But highly organized events can be produced in many ways by one who has the complete art, as we have shown earlier. Consequently, the science of the tragic art cannot be demonstrated, even partly, from historical events alone, for these can function only as individual premises, and from such premises no conclusion is logically possible. It remains, then, that in general and in the tragic art in particular, one can produce an indefinite number of works of art of the same kind either by his or her nature in accord with the scientific principles of that art, as we have discussed at length in Aristotle's Theory of Art, Part III, or, if one does not possess that nature, by learning that art from an artist or a scientist scientifically with the aid of induction and abstraction. Production of tragedies of the best kind, of course, requires knowledge and understanding of human nature, for the construction of probable or necessary events without such knowledge and understanding is practically impossible.

15

1. It is a mistake to translate the Greek word χρηστός (= "*chrestos*") as "good," as some translations do. Such translation would portray all agents in a tragedy as good or virtuous, including slaves and murderers and villains, and this is unacceptable. Even translating that term as "good of its kind" is unacceptable, for this would be ambiguous. The sentence which follows in the text makes Aristotle's meaning clear. An English term which brings out the meaning may be the word "effective" or "cogent" or "credible" or "convincing." Thus an agent in a tragedy is said to be portrayed cogently if his speech and *actions* reveal clearly to the audience his intentions, for these manifest his ethical habits, which constitute his character. We shall use the term "cogent" as the translation of the term "*chrestos*."

2. 1450b8–10.

3. Aristotle regarded *men* as being for the most part superior by nature to women in leadership and intellect (1254b13–14, 1259a39–b3).

4. 1260a33–36.

5. The agent's *actions* and speech should be appropriate to him or her. It would not be appropriate to portray a slave by nature as discussing philosophy with a philosopher or the definition of democracy with a political scientist, for such discussions would be beyond the slave's mental abilities. According to Aristotle, a slave by nature, a moron for example, is a person who inherited a weak intellect at birth and cannot partake of citizenship in a good state; a slave by convention, on the other hand, depends on customs or laws which should not exist in good states, for such a person may be intelligent (1252a24–5b15) and so not a slave by nature.

6. 1448a6, 13, 1453a2–7. Perhaps the term "similar" allows for such character of agents in tragedies as described in legend; for, just as the main events in legendary stories should be kept (1453b22–25), so should the characters of the leading agents as described in those stories. This appears to be suggested by lines 1454a33–36, 1460b32–61a4.

7. Menelaus' baseness of character in the *Orestes* is not necessary in the plot and hence not convincing. This appears to be an example of Rule (1) in the text.

8. In the *Scylla*, perhaps a dithyramb by Timotheus, the lamentation of Odysseus is not suitable to his character as a wily warrior. In the *Wise Melanippe* by Euripides, while Melanippe's father was away,

she bore twins by Poseidon. Upon her father's return, seeing a cow suckling the twins, he regarded it as a bad omen and ordered Melanippe to burn the twins. To save the twins, Melanippe used the accepted physical theories of the origin of things, i.e.,that like begets like, to argue that a cow could not give birth to humans. The two examples violate Rule (2) in the text, for the *action* or speech in each example is not suitable to the agent.

9. This inconsistency does not become Iphigenia, for she is not consistently inconsistent. Rule (4) is violated.

10. Having laid down four desirable attributes of the agent's character, Aristotle now proceeds to show how the last attribute—consistency—is related to an event in which such consistency plays a role in a good tragedy. This procedure in the text is consistent with Aristotle's method. Consistency in character must be discussed before a relation of such consistency to an event is discussed, because that relation is an attribute of consistency but is not implied solely by the nature of that consistency, and as such an attribute it presupposes the existence and the knowledge of that subject, i.e., of consistency (1019a4–6). It is evident, then, that in this sentence we are still discussing character, for the relation of character's consistency to an event belongs to that consistency and hence to the character as the subject of such consistency.

The above paragraph shows also that, contrary to the opinions of many critics, lines 1454a37–b8 which follow immediately neither break the continuity of Aristotle's *thought* nor belong to some other part of the *Poetics*.

11. Is this part of the sentence superfluous? Perhaps not. If events are to proceed necessarily or probably, not only an agent's character must be consistent and the like, but also the resolution should be of a certain kind, i.e., must come out necessarily or probably.

12. *Deus ex machina* in poetry is an artificial means or device introduced, usually by a bad poet, to avoid a difficulty in reaching a desired end. It takes such a form as a miracle or an improbable event or a god's command or intervention, such as the chariot drawn by dragons in *Medea*.

13. Devices based on legend, folklore and the like may be used occasionally for events outside the tragedy (1461a1–4).

14. It appears that Aristotle would prefer plots without any unreasonable events, but he would accept as a second choice such events if

they are just mentioned or implied but are outside the tragedy. Such events are recounted in the *Oedipus Rex* but are not parts of the *action* in the tragedy.

15. 1452b30–53a17.

16. A person who is easily angered may be represented as stern or righteously indignant; for one who is righteously indignant has something in common with one who is irascible, even if the former is not blamed whereas the latter is blamed. Similarly, a fair–minded person has something in common with a person who is slow to anger; for, fair–mindedness requires understanding and taking account of the whole situation and hence takes time; but fair–mindedness is a virtue, whereas slowness to anger is not a virtue but tends to border on insensitivity or lack of personal pride.

17. If tragedy is to be read, stagecraft as an art is not needed; but if it is to be staged, the effects of stagecraft should be anticipated by the poet. The poet should make sure not to omit parts which must be included in a tragedy but should avoid introducing parts which cannot be well staged; for the aim of stagecraft is to enliven tragedies and not lessen their pleasurable effects.

18. Perhaps Aristotle is referring to his work *On Poets*, or to some other related work for the general public.

16

1. 1452a29–32.

2. A quotation from some unknown poet.

3. The 'stars' were the birthmarks of the descendants of Pelops.

4. Odysseus showed his scar to the swineherds to convince them of his identity. His recognition by the nurse was better, for it was the custom for a guest who brought good news to be washed by servants.

5. The recognition in a good tragedy, being an event, should occur as a necessary or probable consequence of the preceding events and not be accidental or an artificial device used by the poet to avoid a difficulty.

6. Tereus, king of Thrace and married to Pandion's daughter Procne, later had intimate relations with Procne's sister Philomela later; and to prevent Philomela from revealing this affair to Procne, he tore her tongue out. But Philomela used the shuttle to weave on her loom words which revealed to Procne Tereus' unfaithfulness. This recognition hardly differs from that in which Odysseus made himself known to the swineherds.

7. *Odyssey*, Book 8, 521 sqq. In both examples, recognition of the agent is caused by the agent's response (i.e., bursting into tears) to remembrance of a past event.

8. *Choephoroi* 166–234, by Aeschylus. Electra, finding a lock of hair similar to hers, infers that her brother has come.

9. Iphigenia would infer from this remark that the stranger is her brother and would stop the sacrifice. It is not known whether the sophist Polyidus suggested this remark as an alternative, or whether as a critic he considered it a better alternative, or whether he was himself a poet. A poet of the same name is mentioned in line 1455b10.

10. Theodectes was a rhetorician and a tragic poet (375–334 B.C.). He wrote fifty tragedies and was an intimate friend of Aristotle. According to Greek legend, Tydeus was the father of Diomedes, one of the bravest heroes of the Trojan War. Nothing more is known of the play *Tydeus*.

11. Nothing more is known of the play the *Phineidae* or of its author or of the legend.

12. Nothing is known of the play *Odysseus the False Messenger* or its author. Apparently, Odysseus purposely committed the fallacy by using the word "know" instead of the word "recognize," thus misleading the characters in the play to think that by "will know" he meant "will recognize," which literally is a synonym of "know again." Was the remark by Odysseus meant to be heard by the audience? Would it make any difference in the play if this were so?

13. Perhaps this refers to lines 1452a24–26 in the *Poetics*.

14. Iphigenia, the priestess of sacrifice, about to sacrifice one of the Greek strangers (Orestes), gave a letter to the other stranger to take to Argos and deliver it to her brother Orestes, asking for her rescue, not knowing that the victim–to–be was her own brother Orestes. The letter was shown to Orestes before the sacrifice, and the recognition followed.

17

1. Since tragedy, unlike epic, is usually written to be performed on stage rather than to be read or recited, certain features which would enhance or be allowed in epic may be unsuitable to a tragedy when performed and so lessen its effect on the audience. The general reason for this is the fact that the content taken in by *thought* through reading or hearing epic (and even tragedy) is universal and so without the presence or absence of the particular elements which vision would sense;

but such elements appearing on stage may be unsuitable or favorable to vision and lessen or add to, respectively, the effect of tragedy on the audience. The writer of tragedy, then, has an added task: he must find ways to guard against the presence in tragedy of unsuitable elements or to introduce favorable elements which enhance tragedy.

2. Nothing is known of the particular incidents in the play itself, whose title is thought by some to have been "*Amphiaraus*." According to legend, Amphiaraus was a seer and prince of Argos. Foreseeing disaster in a war against Thebes, he refused at first to join, but his wife, Eriphyle, bribed by Polynices with a death–causing necklace, persuaded him later to go. Knowing his doom, he bade his sons Alcmaeon and Amphilochus to avenge his death upon Eriphyle. Alcmaeon carried out his father's vengeance after the war.

The text here may be interpreted in two ways: (a) the return from the temple was presented on stage but failed miserably because its performance was by its nature incongruous or absurd, as Achilles' pursuit of Hector in the *Iliad* would have been (1460a11–17); (b) the return from the temple was omitted on stage, thus breaking the continuity of *action* or violating some other principle of the art of tragedy. The text for alternative (a) would be as follows. "The return of Amphiaraus from the temple would have been overlooked had it not been seen by the audience; but on stage it failed miserably, for it displeased the spectators." Most translators use (a); we prefer alternative (b), but either alternative may illustrate Aristotle's point.

3. Suffering is brought about naturally if its appearance implies that suffering is usually caused by actual pain and not by pretended pain or by some other such accidental cause.

4. If performers are to convince the spectators that they suffer, the appearance of their suffering when performing must be the same as the appearance of those who are actually suffering.

5. Poets or performers are said to be naturally gifted if they can mold themselves to any emotion and, although knowing that they are writing or performing, appear to be naturally moved; but they are said to have a touch of madness if, during their performance or writing, they are actually moved but are unaware while being moved that their emotion is not being brought about by its natural cause.

6. The outline of a story is the core or essence of it; that is, it is that part without which the nature or form of the story and hence the story itself will cease to exist or be the same. The other parts may

come or go or vary, but the story itself will still remain the same as long as its essence is not disturbed.

To take a simpler example, the essence of a triangle is to be a three–sided plane figure. Its sides may be or become equal or unequal, great or small, and the same may apply to its angles or area or the like; but these variations or changes do not alter that figure from being still a triangle as long as its essence is not disturbed.

7. If this story is to remain the same, its outline must not change. For example, Euripides and Polyidus gave different versions of the manner in which Orestes was recognized; but the manner in which recognition occurs is not included in the outline, whereas recognition as such is included and kept by both poets, and so both used the same outline and dealt with the same story.

8. Aristotle uses the Greek term *"idion"* in two main senses: it means (a) a property, i.e., that which, not being in the definition of a thing, is demonstrable as belonging to the thing and so belongs to that thing and only to that thing; or, (b) the essence or definition of that thing (101b19–23). In one sense, then, the term *"idion"* functions as a genus of "property" and "essence" and "definition" taken in the primary sense.

18

1. As Lucas says, the term λύσις (= *"lysis"*), which we translate as "resolution," should not be translated as "denouement" as some do, otherwise tragedies whose complications are entirely outside the drama, e.g., the *Oedipus*, would begin with the denouement, contrary to the usual meaning of the term "denouement."

2. It is stated that tragedy includes as a part complication, which in turn includes events outside the drama (assuming "drama" to mean what takes place on the stage). So since such events, being a part of complication and hence of tragedy, have occurred outside the drama and yet are a part of tragedy, they must be a part in the sense that they are mentioned in or somehow implied by the drama as having occurred.

3. If the assumptions made in the preceding Commentary are accepted, then the term "the beginning" which appears in the description of complication would mean the beginning of the drama and not the beginning of past events outside the drama.

4. There seems to be some corruption in the text. The three dots in "bad ... fortune" indicate this. Some translators use "good fortune [or

misfortune]," others use "good fortune ...," others "good fortune or bad fortune." But the change in tragedy cannot be to good fortune, nor to good or bad fortune, nor yet to bad fortune followed by good fortune if it is to be the best tragedy, for a change from bad fortune to good fortune does not end in catharsis of pity and fear and that alternative is inappropriate. In view of the textual difficulty, our choice is made to accord with what Aristotle says about tragedy in other contexts.

5. Some manuscripts include words whose translation is usually given by this bracketed part. The tragedy is not extant.

6. We do not have these plays.

7. Perhaps the Greek terms translated as "involvement" and "complication" are synonyms, or else close in meaning.

8. Things under the same genus are different because of a difference with respect to form and not with respect to matter. So since the part closest to the form of tragedy is the plot, tragedies would be different in virtue of a difference in plot more than in another part; and since involvement and resolution are elements of a plot, tragedies would be the same if these two elements are the same in both of them; but tragedies would be different if at least one element in one tragedy differs from the corresponding element in the other tragedy.

9. 1449b12–20.

10. Perhaps the term "reversal" refers to events in complex tragedies, whereas the term "simple" refers to events without complexity or to the events under the other species of tragedy, whether to some or to all of them (1455b32–56a3).

11. A tragic effect is produced only if the protagonist is the kind of person described in 1452b30–53a12, whereas a feeling of compassion is produced if the protagonist is not such a person, as in the case of Sisyphus and of a brave but unjust person.

12. Improbable events do happen, but they do so occasionally, that is, each kind occurs infrequently, because the different kinds of improbable events exceed by far in number the number of probable or necessary events. The reason for this is that innumerable accidents happen to each thing which exists by nature or of necessity. So, in Aristotle's terminology, it is right to say that things do happen occasionally or accidentally or by accident, but not right to say that they are probable or have probability, if "probability" is used in Aristotle's sense. However, by "having a probability" Agathon meant what modern mathematicians mean when they speak of mathematical probabil-

ity, which ranges from 0 to 1, or from not happening at all to happening always or of necessity.

13. What the chorus does, whether in statement or song, must be in harmony with the events which just precede or are portended, if it is to be a part of tragedy and hence contribute to the tragic effect.

19

1. Of the six parts of tragedy listed in lines 1450a9–10, spectacle and song are not discussed in the *Poetics*; for discussion of spectacle comes under the science of stagecraft, and that of music under the science of music. The proper parts as the subject of the science of tragedy, then, are plot, character, diction and *thought*.

2. The discussion of *thought* rendered through speech comes under the science of rhetoric, which is concerned with the art of persuasion; and the means of the speaker's use of that art, as stated in the *Rhetoric* (1356a1–4), are three: (1) to make a favorable impression on the listeners and so gain their trust,(2) to be able to arouse their emotions, and (3) to convince them through reasoning by using probable or necessary premises or what appear to be probable or necessary premises (1356a1–4). Poetics, then, and particularly the science of tragedy, does not include the art of rhetoric as a subject but must make good use of it in showing how it should be applied to the production of good tragedies.

3. Poetics and rhetoric (as a science) are sciences whose subjects differ. Nevertheless, it is possible for one science to use the results of another science even if it does not investigate the subject of the latter science. It is in this sense that rhetoric may be applied to the science of tragedy. The relations which may exist among the various sciences need not be discussed here.

4. By "that *inquiry*" Aristotle means rhetoric as a science. Rhetoric as a science, it may be added, differs from rhetoric as an art, just as science differs from art; so whenever the term "rhetoric" is used, its meaning should be clear from the context.

5. The term "these" refers to all things concerned with *thought* in tragedy which should be rendered by speech, in which case the three parts (a), (b), and (c) that follow in the translation are concerned with the parts of speech which express *thought* in tragedy and use the truths investigated in (1), (2) and (3), as indicated in Comm. 2 of this

Section. Generally speaking, parts (a) and (b) use truths from (2) and (3), respectively; part (1) is used, but indirectly, e.g., in rendering the agents in a tragedy cogent by means of what they say and do.

6. The terms "maximizing" and "minimizing" as used here are not limited to quantities, or to qualities, or to *actions*, or etc., but may be applied to many categories. One may maximize or minimize the extent or importance or intensity or anything which admits of variation of degree or number or magnitude or importance or priority, etc.

7. The devices meant are the parts (a), (b) and (c) just mentioned in the text.

8. Usually, Aristotle does not repeat completely what is evident from what he has said just previously. We are using "etc." here to indicate what is left out.

9. Events on stage, being observable, need as such no verbal exposition or description; for verbal exposition at best adds nothing but merely repeats what is observed, and at worst it distorts or falls short of or distracts from what is observed. In general, then, observable events on stage *qua* observable should not be verbally stated. But if events on stage are to be related to things which are not observed on stage, the poet may apply the devices mentioned to the things to which those events are so related. For example, if on stage a performer threatens to kill someone, a third performer may urge the first to desist from carrying out the threat, giving as reasons the dire consequences which would or might follow. Here, the impending event is observed as impending, but the consequences are not observed, and those consequences may be maximized to prevent the intended *action*. In short, the tragic poet may use the devices (a), (b) and (c) indicated in the text only for such things as are not observed on stage, regardless of whether those things are or are not related to what is actually observed on stage.

10. The Greek name "*diegesis*" should not be translated as "statement," as it sometimes is. A statement is to a narration as language is to diction; and just as "diction" signifies more than what "language" does, so "narration" signifies more than what "statement" or "language" does.

11. A question and an answer are opposites, and so are an injunction and a prayer. A narration and a threat, however, do not seem to be opposites.

20

1. Since, by definition, tragedy is a poem to be performed, language and hence diction must be used vocally, so diction becomes a part of tragedy in some way; for vocal language is to diction as matter is to form or to the composite of matter and form.

2. Manuscripts differ; in some, the name *"synete"* (= "intelligible") appears, in others, the name *"synthete"* (= "composite"). The correct translation cannot be "intelligible," for Aristotle would have used the Greek word for "significant," which is adequately comprehensive, whereas the Greek word *"synete"* is too limited to cover everything that can be signified by names in general (1142b34–43a18). Besides, mentioning what is or is not significant while discussing letters, which are elements or materials, is not necessary at this stage since such matters are taken up after letters as the ultimate elements of language are treated. It is evident, then, that the correct translation of the Greek word should be "composite."

3. How can a mute, being by definition a letter and hence a vocal sound, be audible? By itself, it is not audible; but it is audible if combined with a letter which is audible. So "to be a vocal sound" signifies to be audible, whether potentially as a part or actually by itself.

4. Perhaps the letter "s" is audible in two senses, potentially as a part, as in "so," or actually by itself, as a hissing sound, which we may write as "ssss... ."

5. The letter "d" cannot be audible by itself at all; but it is audible in the composite syllable "do." Evidently, it is not like the semivowel "s" or "r."

6. Why is there no mention of softness or loudness? If it be said because these two are attributes of voice or sound in general, one may respond that pitch, too, is such an attribute. On the other hand, perhaps pitch and its variations or other attributes are a part of diction, for it often determines the meaning, but volume does not seem to do so, particularly when in relation to another volume.

7. Evidently, the Greek word translated as "syllable" differs in meaning somewhat from the English word "syllable"; for the symbol "gr" would be a syllable in Greek but not in English. On the other hand, there is no better English word for the Greek word, and such translation is in accord with the principles of translation.

8. Corruption and lacunae in the Greek text make it difficult to get

the exact meaning of the Greek name translated here as "connective," and the same applies to the Greek name translated as "joint" in the next paragraph.

9. The Greek name used is "*Theodoron*," in the accusative, in which the part "*doron*" when used by itself is a name which means a gift; but "*doron*" as a part of "*Theodoron*," which is a name of a *man*, has no meaning at all. For convenience, we have used the English name "Fairbanks" in the translation to bring out the same point.

10. Stated more explicitly, both a noun and the corresponding verb have a common root, as in the case of "success" and "succeed"; the meaning of a verb includes time in addition to the meaning of the corresponding noun.

11. By the name "definition," Aristotle means an expression such as "a rational animal" or "three–sided plane figure" and not the statement "a man is a rational animal" and the like. Such expression or definition is called "definiens" by the logicians, and its meaning does not include time.

12. There seems to be a problem. The expression "some parts" in the definition of speech seems to imply that at least two parts of a speech are significant. Here we are told that speech will always have at least one significant part, and this statement seems to allow a speech to have just one significant part, contrary to the definition of speech. Does the expression "some parts" include only *one part* in its meaning?

21

1. Aristotle uses the Greek word "*onoma*" in two senses: it means (1) a noun, and also (2) a word which is a genus that includes nouns, verbs, inflections of these, such as case, tense, comparative and the like, each of which is significant.

2. In the Greek text, the word "*ge*" (= "earth") is used. We use the word "hug" for linguistic convenience, for the part "ear" in "earth" taken by itself is significant, whereas no part of "hug" is by itself significant.

3. In English, perhaps the word "commutation" would be such a double noun, in which the part "mutation" is significant but the part "com" by itself is not; and similarly for the word "reexamine," for the part "re" by itself is not significant. Perhaps the prefixes "com" and "re" are like the Greek conjunctions and joints, which by themselves are not significant.

4. In English, perhaps the word "policewoman" would be such a double name.

5. The Greek word in the text is "*Hermocaicoxanthos*," a shortened composite of the three river names "*Hermos*," "*Caicos*" and "*Xanthos*." The word "megalomaniacology" introduced in the translation, if an English word at all, would have the significant parts "megalo," "maniaco" and "logy," each of these being inflected and together signifying the science of megalomaniacs.

6. Aristotle uses the name "metaphor" in two senses: (1) the name which replaces another name according to the definition just given, and (2) the whole phrase or statement in which the metaphor in sense (1) is present. In the first example which follows, the name "stood" is a metaphor in sense (1), and "there stood my ship" is a metaphor in sense (2).

7. In this example, the name "sowing" applies to seed alone and is defined in terms of "seed" (73a34–b3); but "emitting" is not defined in terms of "flame" because it is more general. So whereas "sowing" is proper to seed, "emitting" is not proper to flame but is applicable to other things also. It is for this *reason* that Aristotle says that there is no one–word name which is limited to the emission of flame from the sun. Alternatives to "flame" are "light," "light rays," "fiery light" and others, for the Greek name used here had many meanings.

8. In this example, the word "cup" is the name belonging to another object, i.e., to Dionysus, and "wineless" is the predicate which may belong to the cup but never to the shield. So since the shield of Ares can never have wine, the phrase "the wineless cup" characterizes the shield more than does the name "the cup."

9. Newly–coined names need not be chosen at random but may have elements which characterize in some way or enhance the subject to which they apply, whether phonetically or with respect to some other form of likeness. The words "sprouter" and "supplicator" for "horn" and "priest," respectively, are such names coined by translators, but other English words may be newly introduced for a horn or a priest.

10. Due to corruption of the Greek text or lacunae or for some other reason, each species of names on the list has been defined except that of ornamental names. We may offer an interpretation and then give a definition of an ornament. It is reasonable to assume that Aristotle was familiar with all the possible species of names or phrases which a poet

might use to enhance the diction of a poem, and it is evident that the various species he gave and defined are mutually exclusive, for Aristotle usually avoided duplication. We are seeking, then, a species called "ornament" which usually excludes all the other species.

Now it is possible for a thing which is an individual or whose name is standard to be called by a phrase or another name that signifies that thing and only that thing. For example, "man" is the standard name for man, but "political animal" and "rational animal" are also predicates of man and of man alone. Similarly, but in a qualified way, George Washington (the historical statesman) may also be called "the first president of the United States." In general, then, a subject's property which enhances the diction of that subject may be preferable to the standard name of that subject if it is used in a poem or in any other speech that aims at effect. Accordingly, the following definition may be given:

> DEF: An ornament is a name or phrase which, being a property of a thing, enhances the diction of a poem by replacing the standard name of that thing in that poem.

The above definition may be generalized if the word "poem" is replaced by the word "language" whenever the aim of that language is enhancement. Other names often used for such enhancements are "circumlocution," "periphrasis" and perhaps others, depending on the context.

From Lattimore's translation of Homer's *Iliad*, some examples of ornaments are: "The blameless seer" for "Calchas," "The child of Zeus of the Aegis" for "Athene," "Lord of the silver bow" for "Apollo," "Kronos' son the dark misted" and "The lord of Olympus who gathers clouds" for "Zeus." Also, if a dispute had arisen in ancient Greece, the speaker might have said, "If justice need be done for this, let the most just of them all decide," referring to Aristides who had earned the epithet "the just."

22

1. Since Cleophon chooses agents who are average rather than better than average (1448a12), he is consistent in using diction which is proper to such agents, i.e., diction which is lucid and commonplace. But just as the choice in tragedy of agents better than average is better than

Cleophon's choice, so will be the choice of the corresponding diction, i.e., of diction which is lucid but dignified rather than commonplace.

2. Sthenelus, mentioned also by Aristophanes, was perhaps a tragic poet.

3. It is assumed that those names are used appropriately, i.e., fittingly and with moderate frequency.

4. Are ornaments strange names? Perhaps some of them sometimes are but others are not. For the definition of a standard name may at times have the effect of spelling out the meaning of that name, and such definition, functioning as a name, would then be a strange name, but in a qualified way, i.e., if it has the effect mentioned, i.e., dignity. To be an ornament, however, is not to be a strange or standard name; for, as logicians would say, two predicates may denote the same thing but they do not necessarily connote the same thing.

5. The word "those" stands for names which are not standard.

6. The name "bronze" is a metaphor for "bronze cup." The reference is to cuppings, in which bronze cups were used on a patient to aid circulation of the blood or to draw blood to the surface of the body.

7. Perhaps the ostentatious use would be the excessive use of strange names, whereas the moderate use would be the proper frequency or quantity.

8. Here, the wrong quality of strange names is added, for such names would not be proper or fitting. So perhaps the word "inappropriate" indicates the wrong quality, whereas the word "deliberate" indicates the excessive and hence the wrong quantity.

9. If the Greek word θοινᾶται (= "feasts on") were a standard name, we would have a metaphor, but according to the text it is a foreign name; so it must have been standard among Greeks who were using a different dialect, for a different name in a different dialect was regarded as a foreign name.

10. In each of the three examples which follow, the first version is evidently better than the second.

11. Manuscripts differ. An alternative to ἀεικής is ἄκικυς. *Odyssey*: 9.515.

12. *Odyssey*: 20.259.

13. *Iliad*: 17.265.

14. Sophocles: *Oedipus Coloneus*, 986.

15. Natural gifts are potentialities or faculties which are inherited

at birth and can be developed, but they cannot be learned by oneself or acquired from others.

16. Perception of similarity or analogy in things, relative to perception of sameness in things, requires greater ability of abstraction, and such ability leads to greater generality and synthesis which are necessary for philosophical thinking.

17. 1406b1–2.

18. Since the emphasis in iambic poems is on imitation of ordinary discourse, forms of diction which tend to lessen imitation should play a minor role. Such forms are expansions of names, contractions, foreign names, and newly–introduced names. The other forms, i.e., standard and metaphoric and ornamental names, consist only of words which are ordinary names.

23

1. The expression "in meter" refers to a single meter, the hexameter; but if not all epics were produced in hexameters, it refers to the hexameter as the appropriate meter for epic (1449b1, 1459b23–7).

2. Dramatic imitation in epic is imitation in which the poet assumes in turn the role of the characters who are imitated, either entirely or almost so, as Homer does (1448a20–22, b34–36, 1460a5–11).

3. 1450b23–27.

4. Since tragedy and epic are compared with respect to excellence, their difference with respect to their end is not a difference in kind but in degree; hence they differ in how well they succeed in achieving the same end.

5. A historical account of events or *actions* that one or many persons did or suffered during one period does not imply a single end, for actual events or *actions* are individuals, and many of them are usually unrelated to each other and have different ends, unlike the events in a good tragedy or an epic, which has a single end.

6. If two or more simultaneous events may be unrelated to each other or have no single end, so may two or more successive events. The argument is from similars to similars, or better, from similars to those which are less similar or not even similar.

7. The name "historian" here is general; it includes one who writes a biography or a history of a nation or an account of the actual events during some period of time and the like. Such an historian may still

make a selection, but the things selected may not have a unity, whether according to probability or necessity or by having a single end.

8. 1451a22–29.

9. If the parts of an *action* do not all follow according to probability or necessity, there is less unity, if a unity at all; and if they do follow and form a whole but are too numerous, the audience may fail to grasp their unity or keep them in memory. These two points are illustrated by the examples which follow.

24

1. The expression "the same species" indicates the kind of species rather than their number, but the list of species given appears to specify both the kinds and the number of species. According to this sentence, then, it would appear that the fourth species of tragedy, not specified for some reason earlier in lines 1456a2–3, would be that of simple tragedy. This is also evident from the fact that some tragedies have neither reversal nor recognition.

2. Of epics, only those which are complex would have reversals or recognitions or both.

3. *Thought* and diction should be beautiful in every epic. The addition of this sentence at this part of the paragraph also seems to imply that the fourth species of epic cannot be an epic of *thought* or of diction.

4. This sentence implies that the same epic may come under two or perhaps more species. Thus the four species mentioned above need not be mutually exclusive. Accordingly, we would have to say that there are two kinds of species, those which are mutually exclusive and those which are not. Perhaps we should use the general word "kind" and say that there are four kinds rather than four species of epic. In fact, the Greek word "*eidos*" was used in many senses, two of which were the two just mentioned.

5. This sentence confirms what was stated in Comm. 3 of this Section.

6. 1451a3–15.

7. Such length of an epic would be equal to the combined length of about three or four tragedies of acceptable length in Aristotle's time.

8. The statement "nature herself teaches poets to choose the fitting meter" is a metaphor which needs clarification. Now the nature of a thing is primarily its form; so by "nature" in that statement Aristotle means a form, more specifically, perhaps man's form, which is man's soul, not the whole soul but a part of it which distinguishes man from

the other animals. That part is man's rationality, which is capable of knowing and understanding things, as stated at the beginning of the *Metaphysics* (980a21). Consequently, knowledge of the fitting meter for epic poems is acquired first by a part of the rational nature (i.e., by the gift) of those who grasped that meter and then taught it to others.

An alternative specification of the meaning of "nature" is the form of epic itself; for if the form of epic is such that it admits only the hexameter to be best appreciated, then gifted poets will perceive it and teach it to others. In either case, discovery of that meter is like other such discoveries. For example, the discovery that a straight line segment can be bisected requires two natures: (a) the nature of a mathematician who has a gift of discovery and (b) the nature of a straight line segment which has the potentiality of being bisected.

9. Poets are imitators of events to the extent that they narrate dramatically, i.e., to the extent that they impersonate the agents in their poems.

10. What is stated as being true but defies reason is more likely to be believed and produce wonder if not observed than if actually observed, and whatever produces wonder is pleasant and often makes us seek the *reason* for the alleged truth. In view of this, epic, whose events are narrated, can produce such wonder more than can tragedy, whose events on stage are observed.

11. For example, the truth "X is a dog" implies the truth "X is an animal," but the truth "X is an animal" does not necessarily imply the truth "X is a dog"; for X may be a horse or some other animal and not a dog. The kinds of false reasonings which a poet should introduce in a poem, however, should not be obvious like the example just given, but rather deceptive and so tending to be plausible.

12. It is not clear whether Aristotle is referring to Penelope's false reasoning or to Eurycleia's, for both appear to be examples of fallacies. In the first example, accepted by Bywater and others, the stranger (i.e., Odysseus) described correctly the clothes of Odysseus at the end of his story in order to convince Penelope that he was telling the truth about having met Odysseus in Crete. The second example, on the other hand, contains false reasoning from a consequent to an antecedent and is therefore a fallacy. Eurycleia knew that Odysseus had been wounded as a boy and as a consequence had a scar. The fallacy here goes as follows: if the stranger is Odysseus, he will have a scar on a certain part of the body; the stranger has a scar on the same part of the body; therefore he is Odysseus. But this conclusion

need not be true; for other men may have such a scar. Porphyry appears to be right in accepting the second example rather than the first as the fallacy. In the first example, the antecedent and the consequent are temporal; but a fallacy requires logical instead of temporal antecedents and consequences, and the mention of the Bath Scene seems to point to Eurycleia.

25

1. A problem is an expression of the general form "Whether A is X or not"; it is posed for discussion and solution, and its solution is used to arrive at truth, whether for its own sake or for the sake of pursuit or avoidance (104b1–3, 105b19–25). If truth is used for its own sake, the aim is (a) knowledge, especially scientific knowledge; if used for the sake of pursuit or avoidance, the aim or proper end may be either (b) *action*, which is for its own sake, or (c) a product, which is usually for the sake of something else. These three ends are the same in kind as those pursued by the three kinds of sciences, namely, the theoretical, the practical and the productive, respectively. In poetics, the aim of truth is for the sake of a good poem, the poem being the product while a person's appreciation of that poem is the final end.

2. Here, again, Aristotle tries to make his meaning of the word "imitation" clearer by a process which he calls "from what is more clear to us but not by nature, to what is more clear to us by nature" (71b33–72a5). This process amounts to starting from what we know about a thing and proceeding to what we should know of it, or from our inadequate knowledge about it to scientific knowledge of it. Thus, the word "imitation" is clearer to us if, as Aristotle says, paintings are used as examples. To get Aristotle's meaning of that word, we are further told that we should include also ideal things, objects as men think or have thought that they are or should be, and occasionally unreasonable or even impossible objects if such objects enhance the function of a poem.

3. The reference is to the kind of language the poet may use to present his imitation to the audience. In other words, he is granted what is known as poetic license. Such license is not granted to the scientist, whose aim is scientific truth unaccompanied by poetic enhancements, which often cloud such truth.

4. The correctness of the poetic art depends on its final cause; but that cause is not identical with the final cause of the political art. The final end of the political art is the happiness of the citizens of the state

to the extent that this is possible, whereas the final end of the poetic art is primarily that part of the citizens' happiness which is served by entertainment or an enjoyable relaxation.

5. For example, if in a tragedy a poet makes an error by using as the protagonist someone whose virtue is less than average, the function in that tragedy will be impeded, and the mistake is essential; for a principle of the tragic art is violated. But if in a tragedy the poet imitates incorrectly the manner of healing a wounded man, a principle of the art of medicine is violated, and the error is said to be accidental or indirect. In general, essential errors are more serious than accidental errors, and accidental errors can best be avoided if the artist seeks guidance from the right sources, i.e., from the arts or the corresponding scientific truths which might be violated.

The above statements are general and so applicable in a similar manner to poems of other species.

6. Since the function of a poem is its end or final cause, and since it is the end which specifies the means but not conversely, the means should be subordinated to the end. Hence means which enhance the right ends may be used to produce good poems. One kind of such means may be an impossibility, especially when it is plausible to a reader or listener, if not to a spectator, as in the pursuit of Hector.

7. The qualification made in this sentence would do away with the use of an impossibility in a tragedy under certain circumstances. For if a tragedy which is enhanced by an impossibility could be enhanced just as well or even better by devices which avoid the impossibility, it would be a mistake to use the impossibility.

8. To paint a female deer with horns violates a truth in zoology, but inability to paint well violates the requirements of the art of painting, for skill in painting is a part of the art of painting, and in painting well both skill and knowledge of the truths according to which skill must proceed are required.

Unlike mathematics, whose principles are few and accurate and hence knowledge of it hardly uses principles from other sciences, except from philosophy and logic, tragedy is concerned with human *actions*, and true statements about them usually require knowledge from many other arts and sciences, most of whose principles do not possess the high degree of accuracy enjoyed by mathematics. In view of this, the poet is likely to make some errors which do not belong to the poetic art, unless he or she has vast knowledge of other arts and sciences. But since the aim of the poetic art is mainly that of producing tragedy and not discovering scientific truth, errors which do not violate the poetic art may have little effect on the final end of poems and are not serious unless they are too obvious, and it is just for critics not to be too rigorous about problems concerning accidental errors.

9. In portraying characters or events, a poet may do so in any of the three possible ways: either (a) truly, i.e., as they are or were in life, or (b) ideally, i.e., as they should be at best, or (c) according to men's statements or opinions or tradition about them, whether in the past or at present. So if the critic thinks that the poet failed to use alternative (a), the response or solution would be that the end of tragedy or epic may also be attained by choosing (b) or (c). Similarly, the choice may be (a) or (c), but not (b), and it may be (a) or (b), but not (c). In short, the important point is not whether the choice is (a) or (b) or (c), but whether the final end of a tragedy or an epic or any other poem is best attained regardless of the choice, as in problems (1) and (2) in the translation.

10. To evaluate in a poem an agent's *action* or speech, one should attend not only to the *action* as such or to the speech as such, but also to the circumstances under which the *action* was performed or the speech was made. For, since the agents in a poem differ in character, assuming that they are cogently portrayed, they differ also in the *actions* they are expected to perform, for differences in character cause differences in *actions* habitually performed; and the same applies to speech. Similarly, the time when the *action* was performed or the speech was made or the victim upon whom the agent *acted*, and the purpose for acting or speaking or the extent or degree to which these were done, etc., should be considered. A speech or an *action* is only one element and hence only one part of a situation taken as a whole, and since the function of a part must be referred to the function of the whole, the goodness or badness of the part, too, must be referred to the goodness or badness of the whole. It follows, then, that one should attend first to the function and hence the goodness or badness of the whole before making an evaluation of a part.

11. Concerning diction, one must first grasp the meaning that the poem intends, for failure to do so leads to unjustifiable censure.

12. 1457b6–13. *Iliad*, 10. 11–13.

13. *Odyssey*, 5. 275. The reference is to the constellation the Great Bear, which in northern latitudes never sets and hence never partakes 'in the baths of Ocean.'

14. A falsehood attributed to Zeus in Agamemnon's dream would be attributed to someone else by a change in intonation.

15. The reference is to a part of something made of oak, a kind of wood which is least likely to rot.

16. In (a), the things were first mixed, but later became unmixed; in (b), the things were first unmixed, but later became mixed. So we have to choose between (a) and (b). The problem is caused by the absence of punctuations in the ancient Greek texts. What is the solution?

Some knowledge of the views of ancient philosophers may help. The ultimate elements of things are immortal, i.e., indestructible; the composites of these elements are mortal, i.e., destructible, for sooner or later composites will be decomposed and lose their form or nature. But elements are prior in existence to composites; for if composites exist, so do their elements, but if those elements exist, the composites need not exist and so are posterior in existence and are generated later in time; and some ancient philosophers attributed priority in time and existence to the elements over the composites. In view of such belief, one has to choose (b) for consistency, and in English texts a comma or something equivalent should follow rather than precede the word "before." Plato, in describing the nature of things, considered the principles and elements as being the *One* as form and the *Dyad* as matter and the *Ideas* as being composites of these, and he talked of the composites as if they had been generated ultimately from those two principles (991b2–3, 1084a2–7).

17. The ambiguity can better be indicated if we add the bracketed part which is in Homer's text. The word "more" in the translation is ambiguous because the meaning of the text is not spelled out. If "more than two parts of the night" refers to more than two–thirds of the night, then less than one–third of the night is left, and this cannot be the meaning; but if it refers to more than one of the two parts of the night, i.e., more than half of the night, and if this were no more than two–thirds of the night, there would be no inconsistency. There are other ways of evading the inconsistency.

18. The kind of diction meant appears to be one adopted by custom. The name that a poet uses is still standard, although the meaning given to it by custom is not wholly literal, but partly so; yet a critic might still object. In the examples given, such are the names "wine," which means a mixture of wine and water, "tin," which means an alloy of tin

and copper, "bronze–workers," which means workers of iron, and "Zeus's wine–server," which means a server of nectar but not of wine.

19. Here, too, it is by custom that many meanings have been assigned to a name, and the poet may answer that the critic failed to grasp the correct meaning.

20. In the example, a slight mistake in spelling of a man's name gave rise to the unjustified censure. The name of Penelope's father was not "Icarius," the Spartan, but "Icadius," the Cephallenian; so how could Telemachus meet his grandfather Icadius in Sparta?

21. In answering a critic who censures a poet for using an impossibility, the poet may use either of the two senses of "impossibility" (280b12–14).

22. The solution, as stated earlier, is that sometimes a plausible impossibility is better than an implausible possibility because it enhances the function of the poem.

23. The solution is that the ideal, even if impossible or unattainable, (a) is better than the real, (b) renders the poem more beautiful, and (c) satisfies the soul's wishes (1460b1–2).

24. In justifying the use of an unreasonable object, the poet may say that such is or was the general opinion and that, even if the unreasonable is improbable, it still has a *mathematical* probability of existing, albeit a small one.

25. Concerning the appearance of an inconsistency, the poet may answer by using any of the linguistic devices already mentioned or any of those listed in the *Sophistical Refutations* (164a20–184b8). The mention of a prudent person refers to such matters whose decision requires prudence, which includes knowledge of the ultimate final causes (1140b20–1). So to censure a poet who chooses something which in itself is harmful is not necessarily justified, for the reason for such choice may be the prevention of greater harm.

26

1. The argument, with added premises, may be stated as follows. Since the less vulgar poem is the better form, and since the better form is addressed to the better class of spectators, who are relatively few, the form which is addressed to all kinds of spectators would tend to please the majority of spectators, who are not the better class but are rather common people, and such form is in bad taste. If, in the bracket, we replace the word "spectators" by the word "objects," a similar argument follows.

2. Such things are very frequent. See *Hamlet*, III, ii, lines 1–16.

3. The new school favored tragedy; the old school favored epic.

4. A cultivated spectator in the poetic art is one who has good taste in matters of such art, i.e., who is a good judge in discriminating good from bad works of the poetic art.

5. A rhapsodist in ancient Greece was one who recited epic poems or parts of them. The profession of a rhapsodist was analogous to that of a tragic performer on stage. Since the art of tragedy differs from the art of performing tragedy, a bad performance of a tragedy does not imply that the tragedy is bad, and the same applies to the art of epic. See Plato's *Ion*. Consequently, one's argument against a tragedy by referring it to bad performance has no basis.

6. The fact that bad movements are observed often in performances of tragedies but not in epics is no argument against tragedy, for movement may be good or bad in tragedy, just as it is good or bad in dancing or any other kind of poem.

7. Tragedy produces its effect by being read as well as by being performed on stage, just as epic does by being read as well as by being recited by a rhapsodist.

Evidently, the arguments in (1), (2) and (3) in the text should not be used in comparing tragedy with epic. Arguments (4), (5), (6) and (7) which follow, on the other hand, favor tragedy over epic.

8. The essential parts of epic are plot, character, *thought* and diction; and these are parts of tragedy also. Tragedy as performed includes also spectacle and song (1450a7–10).

9. Vividness in presentation is more pronounced in tragedy than in epic.

10. Other things being equal, a poem which has more unity is better than a poem which has less unity; for that which has less unity tends to the indefinite and to matter and hence to be unknowable, whereas that which has more unity tends to the definite and to form and to be knowable, and, among things which are good, that which is definite and a form and knowable is better than that which is indefinite and matter and unknowable.

ARISTOTLE'S THEORY OF ART

PART I: *PROBLEMS*

What is poetics? In order to understand the meaning Aristotle gave or would have given to the term "poetics" and the subject to which that term would apply, we can do no better than turn to his *Poetics* itself. Although no definition of poetics appears explicitly in that work or in the other extant works, nonetheless, from his general methodology and from the *Poetics* itself a definition can be induced. Having arrived at this definition, we may then turn to the aim of poetics and of the *Poetics* in particular.

Almost all of Aristotle's works which have come down to us were written scientifically, and from this fact one might infer that the *Poetics* would be a science. But since Aristotle's definition of art includes the genus "true reason" (1140a9–10), whose definition according to him includes "scientific knowledge" as a species, one might also infer that the *Poetics* would be an art or perhaps a work of art. Whether Aristotle regarded poetics as a science, or an art, or a work of art, or a theory about art, or literary criticism about works of art depends partly on his definitions of these human achievements and on their relation to each other, if any. Consequently, his definition of science, of art, and of the others should be considered before his definition of poetics is stated.

In going over the text of the *Poetics*, the reader is also faced with the problem of understanding the meaning Aristotle assigns to some terms he uses and of knowing the methods he employs. Only a few of the key terms used in that work are defined or made clear, but most of the others are appropriately defined or discussed in his other works, where they belong. For example, anger and pity and fear are defined in the *Rhetoric*, art and happiness in the *Nicomachean Ethics*, nature and luck in the *Physics*, scientific knowledge in the *Posterior Analytics*, and a principle and a cause in the *Metaphysics*. It appears, then, that accurate knowledge of the *Poetics* presupposes knowledge of some parts of the other works, for that knowledge may forestall misinterpretation, which often leads to verbal arguments, and apparent disagreements or contradictions. For this reason, whenever advisable, we provide references, add commentaries, and include a glossary at the end. As for the methods used here, many if not most are present in all of Aristotle's scientific works; perhaps they were considered scientifically in his lost work, the *Methodics* (1356b19). We shall be making some comments on them in the Commentaries.

Another problem is the text itself. There are many variants and many lacunae in the manuscripts that have come down to us, and even the order of some parts is questioned by some translators. In view of these difficulties, translators are often tempted to give interpretations, some of which are not consistent with Aristotle's statements in his other works.

PART II: *THE NATURE OF SCIENCE*

What is science according to Aristotle? Science is fully discussed in the *Posterior Analytics*, but here we shall use only what is needed to understand Aristotle's theory of art and his *Poetics*. The fundamental concepts considered in that treatise are those of science and of scientific knowledge of a fact; the latter is defined explicitly (71b9–12), and the former can be defined in terms of scientific knowledge of a fact and what is implied by that knowledge.

> DEF: Scientific knowledge of a fact is general knowledge of a fact acquired by a demonstration of it, i.e., by a proof through its cause (71b9–12, 1086b33).

This definition may be clarified by certain of Aristotle's assumptions and by examples. Knowledge of a fact is assumed to be true *thought*, and the contrary of that knowledge is mistaken knowledge, or better, false *thought*. It is assumed that a fact exists or can exist (76b3–11). Examples of general knowledge are a clear knowledge of a triangle, as stated in its definition, and the *thought* corresponding to the expression "gold sinks in water," which is a truth about every instance of gold and has the same meaning as the *thought* corresponding to the expression "every instance of gold sinks in water."

According to the above definition, a demonstration in a science is a proof of a theorem through the cause. But what is a cause? It is an answer to the question "Why?" For example, one may ask, "Why does gold sink in water?" The cause in this case is given by the minimum part of the nature or attributes of gold which is necessary and sufficient for the sinking of gold in water (73b25–4a3). Is the yellow color of gold necessary for the sinking? Certainly not, for things which are not yellow, too, may sink in water, as in the case of steel. In the case of gold, it is its specific gravity, which is greater than 1, that causes it to sink. The syllogism then would be as follows: "Gold has a specific gravity greater than 1; whatever has a specific gravity greater than 1 sinks in water; therefore gold sinks in water." Briefly, then, scientific knowledge of a fact is true, general, includes its proof through the cause, and is knowledge of what exists or can exist (100b5–8). Aristotle uses the term "cause" in four different senses; as to the kind of cause or causes which should be given in a demonstration, we need not discuss it here.

Let us now turn to Aristotle's definition of a science, which can be induced from the *Posterior Analytics*.

> DEF: A science is scientific knowledge of facts coming under one sub-ject, whether this be one genus of things or one general aim, and includes (1) principles (concepts, definitions, axioms, and hypotheses) arrived at by various methods, such as sensation, abstraction, experience, and induc-tion, and also (2) demonstrations of demonstrable truths (i.e., of theorems) from those principles; and general knowledge is true either (a) of neces-sity and hence universally, or (b) for the most part, i.e., in most cases or ap-proximately (71a1–100b17, 1003b10–20, 1065a4–5).

The above two definitions concerning sciences imply many attri-butes, some of which may help the reader to better understand Aristotle's theory of art and the *Poetics*.

1. Science is impossible without sensation, experience, abstraction, and other methods which are needed to arrive at its principles (81a38–b9).

2. The principles of a science must be true, either necessarily, as in logic, or approximately, as in political science (71b19–23, 96a8–19, 1027a20–22).

3. Primarily, science is knowledge and hence exists in the mind; secondarily, science exists in symbolic form, e.g., in books. Symbolic knowledge exists ultimately for the sake of knowledge in the mind, but not conversely (16a1–9).

4. A science has unity if and only if it is concerned with one general subject, which may be either one genus of things, e.g., plants in the case of botany, or one general aim, e.g., victory in the case of strategy in war (1003b12–15).

5. One science may be more accurate than another if its principles are fewer, or if its subject is less vague, or if more of its principles have been demonstrated than left undemonstrated (87a31–37, 96a8–19).

6. Some principles are common to all sciences or to many sciences; other principles are proper to each science (77a26–31).

7. A theorem is a conclusion proved through the cause that a property belongs to a subject. Such proof is called "demonstration."

8. No theorem in one science can be a theorem in another science; but a theorem in one science may be *used* by another science or *be applied* to another science. For example, theorems in mathematics can be applied to physics (71b19–23, 75a38–b6, 847a24–28).

9. Every theorem in a science is general; for all principles in a science are general, and from general principles as premises only general conclusions or theorems can be demonstrated. Consequently, a science is not concerned with any individual but can be applied to an individual.

10. The sciences are infinite in number (170a22–23). Consequently, the growth of scientific knowledge cannot come to an end.

From the list of attributes of a science just given it should be evident that Aristotle's concept of a science hardly differs from the concept of a science as understood today. New sciences have been introduced since Aristotle's time, and new theorems have been demonstrated, but the concept of a science has remained about the same. Further, the fact that some of the hypotheses held by Aristotle turned out to be false on better evidence—something that happens to scientists even today—does not change the truth of his assertion that the hypotheses in the sciences should be true.

There are three kinds of sciences; all of them seek truth, but for different reasons. Theoretical sciences seek truth for its own sake; two examples are pure mathematics and theoretical physics. Practical sciences seek truth for the sake of *action*, usually as an end in itself; two examples are ethics and political science. Productive sciences seek truth for the sake of producing or making something; two examples are medical science and engineering. A practical or productive scientist, like a theoretical scientist, need not go further than just seek the truths of his science. A political scientist, for example, need not be a statesman or a judge, and a productive scientist need not produce anything; their function is to discover or teach the truths of their disciplines, which others may use.

Those who have acquired the habit of using scientific truths skillfully to make things are usually called "artists." It often happens, too, that the same person is both a scientist and an artist in the same field. The term "scientist," it may be added, has two senses: (a) one who discovers scientific truths, and (b) one who has acquired from others scientific truths. Also, one may seek scientific truth not for the sake of the proper aim of the science acquired but for an accidental aim. For example, one may acquire political science for the sake of gaining power or may become a lawyer for the sake of financial ends.

To avoid linguistic confusion, let the term "thought" signify any idea existing in the mind, whether simple or composite, let the term "concept" signify a simple idea, and let the term "*thought*" signify a composite idea. Since meaningful symbols stand for ideas in the mind, let the word "term" correspond to the word "concept," the word "expression" correspond to the word "thought," and the word "reason" correspond to the word "*thought*". These correspondences may be written as follows:

thought	⟷	expression
concept	⟷	term
thought	⟷	reason

Further, a term may be a noun or a verb or an adjective or an adverb, and reason may be a statement or a definition or a prayer or a command or a novel or any other such composite expression. The term "reason" as described here should not be confused with the term "reasoning," which is used in logic to mean drawing valid conclusions, and the term "rational" should be regarded as a synonym of the expression "ability to use reason" and not of the term "reasonable," for reason may be a false as well as a true statement, and men, although rational, may be unreasonable. We may add, the Greek term transliterated as "*logos*," which we translate as "reason," is often used by Aristotle as a genus of both "reason" and "*thought*" as already described, and we shall use it sometimes in this broad sense and sometimes in the narrow sense.

PART III: *ART*

Let us now turn to Aristotle's theory of art. Since, according to him, by using the same kind of materials, some men produce better works of a given kind than do other men, there must be a science and the corresponding art according to which those works can be produced in the best way. Aristotle asserts that such a science is productive and that it is an artist who can produce works of art from those materials in the best way. An ideal artist, of course, can hardly exist; but let a producer who comes fairly close to an ideal artist be called "artist," and let the terms "art" and "work of art" signify art and work of art, respectively, taken in a sense similar to that of "artist" as just stated.

But what is art as we usually conceive it, what is Aristotle's concept of it, how are the two concepts related, and how is art related to science?

The Greek term τέχνη, transliterated as "*techne*," is usually translated as "art," and Aristotle assigns only one meaning to this term. The English term "art," on the other hand, has many definitions or descriptions according to English dictionaries; but if certain parts of these are selected and put together in a certain way, the meaning of the composite signifies about the same things as does Aristotle's term "*techne*." It appears, then, that "art" should be the translation of "*techne*," for no other English term can come as close in meaning to the meaning which Aristotle assigns to "*techne*." To avoid confusion, let us state Aristotle's definitions of reason, art, artist, work of art, and skill.

> DEF: Reason is a thought or expression with parts, each of which has meaning (1457a23–27).

> DEF: Art, in general, is an acquired skill which enables a man to produce with true reason something which can be produced (1140a1–23).

Let the thing produced by art be called "a work of art," and let a man who produces such a work be called "an artist." Let us also limit the term "production" to the generation of a work of art. The term "making" is often used as a synonym of "production."

> DEF: Skill is a habit which is used in accord with true reason in the production of a work of art.

As suggested in Part II, true reason in the broad sense is true *thought* or the corresponding true statement; as knowledge, it exists in the mind, but as an expression, it exists in symbolic form. For example, the *thought* that men in general like friends corresponds to the statement "men in general like friends," and both the *thought* and the statement are true and are instances of true reason. One kind of true reason, then, exists in the sciences as a true *thought* or statement; such reason may be an axiom or a definition or a hypothesis or a demonstration or a theorem, and each of these is general in character. An artist, too, must use true reason which is general and which he has acquired in order to be an artist.

But there is also another kind of true reason which an artist must use, namely, a true *thought* or statement in which the subject of which something is predicated or to which something belongs or is applied is an individual; and such reason is not general since it is applied to an individual. For example, a carpenter's true reason that the wood he bought to make a walnut chair is walnut and not some other kind of wood is about an individual; he may have said to himself, "This wood is good walnut; I will buy it." So since an artist produces works of art, he or she must use true reason to identify individual objects and deal with them correctly to produce a work of art, which is itself an individual.

An artist may also use in a production what we usually call "rules," and these enable the artist to act correctly in producing a work of art. But what are rules?

In general, rules are of two kinds, those which are man–made and may be changed without affecting the aim, as in playing cards, and those which must not be changed because the change will not bring about the aim. In baseball, for example, three strikes and the batter is out, the aim being to win with a higher score; and the rule may be changed to "four strikes and the batter is out" without affecting the aim, which is winning with a higher score. In moral *action*, on the other hand, the rule may be: "Be just to your friends"; but this rule is based on a truth, namely, "Being just to one's friends usually makes one happier than being unjust to them." In mathematics, too, which is a science, if a term on one side of the equation is transposed to the other side, the rule is to change the sign of that term. If the rule is violated and the sign is not changed, the aim in mathematics, which is demonstrating truths, is frustrated because falsities and contradictions will soon follow. Evidently, the rule to change the sign is based on a truth, whether demonstrable or not, and truths are not man–made but depend on facts. Let us illustrate.

Let $A + 4 = 7$. Transposing 4 to the other side and changing its sign, we obtain $A = 7 - 4$, i.e., $A = 3$. This result can also be obtained by the use of the true axiom on which the rule is based, namely, "If equals be added to equals, the sums are equal," thus:

$$\begin{array}{r} A + 4 = 7 \\ -4 = -4, \end{array} \qquad (1)$$

adding we have $A = 7 - 4$, i.e., $A = 3$.

Here, the rule for transposing is based on the axiom. It is evident from the mathematical illustration above that one may use either the accepted rule, or the true axiom, as in (1); the conclusion is the same.

More often than not, the use of the rule which depends on a truth is more convenient than the use of the truth itself, for it saves time; but if it is not stated why the rule always *works*, those who seek understanding and who desire to go deeper into this matter may wonder why the mere mechanical use of the rule leads to truths or to works of art. Usually, a man who pursues *actions* for their own sake or productions for the sake of the products is less inclined than a scientist or a philosopher to bother with the scientific reasons on which rules depend, especially when he does not need such reasons; but perhaps those reasons should be given or mentioned, at least for the sake of those who seek understanding.

Let us grant, then, that the artist must use true reason which is individual. Must true reason which is general be used in production also? Finding the answer to this question may be facilitated by an examination of the nature of skill. According to the definition, the production of a work of art requires the use of skill, which proceeds in accord with true reason; but it was shown that an artist may use some rules without being aware of the truths upon which those rules are based and still produce a work of art. If so, it would seem that works of art may be produced without the aid of true reason which is general. Indeed, many people hold that artists with great talent and strong intuitions in certain fields, like Homer and Shakespeare and Mozart, do not need knowledge of science or general truths to produce great works of art. Do they speak truly?

The problem is partly resolved if Aristotle's distinction between the two phrases "in accord with true reason" and "with true reason" is made clear. To produce an object *with true reason* is to produce it *with the knowledge* of the true reason which is to be used, and this means that the producer must know the true reason, even if he happens to take a short cut and uses the corresponding rule, which is general; but to produce an object *in accord with true reason* is to produce it but *not necessarily with the knowledge of true reason,* for one may use a rule or some other equivalent, as long as the production as such does not differ from that which is done with the knowledge of the corresponding true reason, for in both cases the product will be the same.

Now skill was defined as a habit which acts in accord with true reason, and a habit is a stable disposition to think or act in the same way under the same or similar circumstances. For example, a sculptor, having skill, is not limited to the production of only one object of some kind but can produce in a similar way an indefinite number of objects of the same kind. Thus the habit of transposing a term of an equation from one side to the other side and changing its sign can be used on an indefinite number of equations, and as such it is analogous to a general and true statement which is predicable of or applicable to an indefinite number of things of the same kind. Similarly, the shoemaker, an artist, can make an indefinite number of shoes of the same kind by using similar operations; so the habit of doing this is analogous to knowledge of a general truth, e.g., to the truth "similar actions on similar objects result in similar products." Finally, true reason as a part of the definition of art is not limited to one individual thing but can be applied to an indefinite number of individuals of the same kind, e.g., to the making of many similar shoes by a shoemaker.

It is evident, then, that the production of a work of art involves, whether explicitly or implicitly (e.g., by the use of rules), two kinds of true reason, individual and general. Thus an artist who produces works of art must *knowingly* use true reason which is individual in producing a single work of art, and he or she must also have the skill which can be used to produce an indefinite number of individuals and which must proceed, *knowingly or not,* in accord with true reason which is general. In view of these facts, the phrase "in accord with true reason" and not the phrase "with true reason" must be used in the definition of skill.

If we may digress a little, the above distinction between "with true reason" and "in accord with true reason" has a number of applications. For one thing, it applies to *actions* and *thoughts,* for one may *act* or *think with* true reason or may do so *in accord with* true reason when he does not know the reason; for another, it applies to education. In both cases, there are times when the use of the rule should be made or precede the use of the corresponding true reason, which is general. For example, children at their early ages are not yet capable of understanding true reason which is general and has an effect on good habits. Making them at first acquire good habits of doing things unknowingly but in accord with true reason is easier and better than speaking to them scientifically or giving them true reasons which are general but not easily understood. As they grow older and their habits, which are being formed in accord with true reason, become more stabilized, they are more capable of understanding and more likely to be convinced of the true reasons behind their activities than if they did not possess those habits.

It was stated earlier that science exists primarily in the mind of the scientist and secondarily as an expression; can it be truly said that art, too, may exist but not necessarily in the mind? Now art requires skill, and skill cannot function unless it exists in the possessor of it. But written or printed expressions do not possess skill and so cannot act; nor can the voice of the artist do so. Does art, then, exist only in the artist? But it appears that art and skill exist also in some animals, like spiders, which spin webs.

On the other hand, animals do not appear to have reason as defined earlier (1332b3–5), for only rational beings are thought to have reason. What animals seem to have is a certain nature or instinct, which is an inborn or natural tendency to behave as a species in a certain manner but not *with reason*, and that is how spiders behave; but, unlike spiders, not all men become by nature artists, e.g., carpenters or composers of music, perhaps because special learning which includes both true reason and training is usually required. Nor can God possess art, for His activity (1074b15–5a10), being continuous and the same and eternal and the best, cannot include or have as its object the production of a work of art; it would indeed be ridiculous to think of God as producing chairs. Finally, we often speak of paintings and statues and other such products as being art or instances of art. In so doing, we are using the term "art" in two senses, i.e., as meaning art, which is an ability as defined, and also a work of art, which is the product made by that ability. But we are speaking of art as an ability, and this is not the things produced. It would seem, then, that art as defined can exist only in an artist, i.e., only in a person who has the skill to produce works of art.

Perhaps the difference between art and nature or instinct should be examined, for some hold that reason or thinking exists in animals other than man, but to a small extent; for the young of some animals are observed to imitate their parents and to be taught by them to do certain things, as in the case of lions and cats, and some animals learn to obey the commands of their trainers, as in the case of dogs and horses. It would seem, then, that animals possess reason.

There is another difficulty; in lines 1451a16–24 Aristotle states that Homer seems to have grasped well, whether *by his nature or by his art*, the fact that a plot in a tragedy may not have unity even if it is concerned with one person only, the implication being that, in producing a work of art, one may grasp a point well either by art or by nature. But if one point in producing a work of art can be grasped by man's nature, other points can be so grasped. So what is the difference between grasping a point by nature and grasping the same point by art, or, a better question, what is the difference between nature and art? If man's nature rather than art can grasp points and produce a work of art, so can a spider's nature, and conversely; for it is by its nature that a spider can produce a web, which appears to be analogous if not similar to a work of art. Moreover, if a person produces a work of art by art, this would appear to mean that a work of art can be produced by man's nature. For art and science come under true reason by definition, since both include true reason. But reason is caused by man's power to reason, and this power, which is usually called "rationality," is a part of man's nature. It should follow, then, that a work of art must always be produced by man's nature or a part of that nature. Then what is art if not caused by nature or a part of nature, and what is nature?

When we speak of the nature of a thing, we usually mean its form (1014b35–5a5), or else its powers which cause the thing's behavior (by "behavior" here we mean mean thoughts and actions and affections in the case of man, but actions and affections in the case of things which do not have reason at all). For example, when we say that all humans by their nature can make statements, we mean that if no part of man's nature or form is damaged or impeded, especially that of using reason, such a person without exception can make statements.

Natures range from those which are simple to those which are complex. Fire's nature is to be hot and to heat, and its heat burns certain things and is quenched by certain other things; and this is universally the case, especially since that nature is simple, although heat, like the sensation of it, admits of variation of degree. A plant, too, has a nature, but one not as simple as that of fire. Since that nature has many parts which may be damaged or impeded in many ways during the plant's existence, a plant may fail to exist normally in many ways. It may grow abnormally or fail to produce fruit or seed. The nature of animals is even more complex, especially that of man. Human nature has some of the higher powers which the other animals cannot possess, and each of those powers usually admits of more variations when in activity than does heat when it acts or is acted upon.

The behavior of all things of a certain kind or species, then, is the realization or fulfillment of the corresponding powers which make up the nature of those things, assuming that no power is damaged or impeded. Thus the heat of fire always burns certain things; and we may add here that fire always burns without knowing it. The actions and affections of plants, too, behave in a similar manner, for they are the realization or fulfillment of the nature or powers of those plants. When we meditate upon the development and ultimate structure of a fruit or a flower, we are struck by the wonders of their nature. Artists may make beautiful paintings and bridges, and poets may write beautiful poems, but all these works of art fade into insignificance when compared with the marvelous processes of a plant's nature, which are at work in the making of a fruit or a flower, even if plants have no knowledge of what they are doing.

Now although the nature of all animals includes the power of sensation as a property of all animals, that is, as an attribute or essential element of all animals but of no other things, the behavior of all animals other than man appears to have shown no perceptible change or progress from generation to generation up to the present, and the same may be said of all plants. But man's behavior has shown a marked change, especially in advancing the sciences and also the arts which require some aid from those sciences. In other words, man has progressed while plants and the other animals have remained static. One may conclude, then, that there must be a cause of man's change or progress; and that cause would be signified by at least a part of the definition of man, namely, by the differentia which is proper to man alone or by a part of that differentia.

The usual definition given of man is "rational animal," and it appears that rationality or the power to acquire (whether by oneself or from others) and to use reason as already defined earlier would be the cause or a part of that cause of man's progress (1253a9–18, 1332b3–8). That reason may be individual or general. And since man's advance in the sciences requires the discovery of new reason which is general, whereas no such advance has been made by the other animals, it follows that those animals do not possess the power of acquiring or using such reason, (1332b3–5), even if one grants that they may acquire individual reason. It follows, too, that they cannot prove a conclusion from premises, for such proof must use at least one premise whose two terms are general. But it appears that they cannot even acquire individual reason, for such reason includes at least one general term, e.g., the term "beautiful," which requires the power of abstraction if it is to be conceived. To imagine one dog saying to another dog "that cat across the street is beautiful" is to live in *Alice In Wonderland*. Moreover, if animals can form one general or abstract term, they can form many and combine them to form general statements, in which case they will be like humans and make some progress like humans. Finally, such animals do not have the organs or cannot use what organs they have to articulate sounds or motions if they are to make any statements. But if they had reason, they would have had the corresponding organs to communicate reason also, for nature does nothing in vain (271a33). They do have, however, the power to receive stimuli and to respond or make sounds to indicate such things as danger, pleasure, and pain, which are useful for their preservation and generation and the like. They tend also to act or respond in a similar manner to similar things, but differently to different things, as dogs do by running to their masters but barking at strangers. Some of them do learn some things from man, as in circuses and mazes in laboratories, whether by imitation or in some other way, but they cannot transmit it from one generation to another. Clearly, then, man has the power to acquire and use true or false reason, both individual and general, but the other animals cannot acquire reason at all.

Let us now return to the problem that was posed earlier, namely, whether it is possible for one person to produce a work of art by art but for another person to produce the same work of art by nature. If it is possible, the problem of whether one can be a great artist without knowing much science can also be answered. We have shown that all animals other than man are deprived of any reason; so their behavior must be caused by the kind of powers they possess—another way of saying that it must be caused by the powers inherited at birth and developed later, that is, by their mature nature. Further, every member of a given species of such animals behaves in about the same way by its nature as the other members do, so certain kinds of distinctions which are observed in humans and which are due to art—for example, one person is a cook, another a poet, another a musician, etc.—hardly exist in those animals. It follows, then, that such distinctions in people must be caused by variations in a power proper to the human species, namely, by variations in rationality. So, in one way, one may truly say that whatever someone does or suffers is caused by his or her nature or a part of that nature, for it is caused by a power which one inherits as a member of the human species, and that power is rationality, i.e., the ability to acquire and use reason; in another, one may truly say that if the kind of power which someone fulfills is not shared by all the members of the human species but only by few, not everything that an individual may do or suffer is caused by the rationality which is common to the nature of all humans.

For example, of those who pursue mathematics, some learn it from others with difficulty; others learn it from others with ease but have no research ability; still others learn it with ease and can also do mathematical research. The same happens to powers of music, for some cannot but others can produce symphonies. Evidently, the originality or creative ability or genius of the last group in each of these examples is not shared by all the members of the human species but is inherited by that group and is a property of that group alone and not of the other members. Consequently, of those who possess mathematical knowledge, some acquired it from others but have no research ability, others have acquired some of it by themselves because of their research ability. We speak of the latter group as endowed with a gift, but of the first group as not possessing such a gift. Gifts such as research ability are inherited and may develop but are not acquired from others. In the arts, too, we say that some are natural athletes but others require instruction and much practice to become athletes, and that Michelangelo and Mozart and Shakespeare had great gifts, evidently because they had inherited and developed them, whereas most people have no such luck.

Some people, then, can produce certain works of art either (a) with the aid of their special nature, i.e., an inherited gift, if that gift is a power only of those few who possess it and not of the human species as a whole, or (b) by art, i.e., if that gift is lacking, but those without it, as members of the human species, i.e., with ability to acquire from others and to use reason, have learned from others the corresponding art of producing works of that art. In view of this difference, Aristotle's remark, that Homer was a great poet either by nature or by art, becomes understandable. Aristotle was inclined to think that Homer's greatness was due more to his own gift of producing great poems than to instruction he had received from others.

But let us be more specific about rationality as a power which has variations. Since all humans are by nature rational but some can contribute to progress while others cannot, it is evident that what is common to all humans and a property of all of them as a unit is rationality at its minimum; and this is exactly the kind which cannot contribute to progress. Those who contribute to progress, then, have additional parts of rationality, and these parts vary in a great many ways, for progress may vary in quantity, quality, degree, and kind. In quantity, progress needs no explanation, for any new research or new and better methods of discovery or production in science or art, respectively, increases progress. In quality, a principle of a science or an art (1098b6–8), for example, certainly surpasses a consequence which follows from it (183b22–25), for principles are difficult to perceive or invent, and without them no theorems or new productions are possible (1098b6–8). In degree, differences certainly exist, for degree is an attribute of some qualities, and improvements in quality are possible. In kind, there can be as many generic and specific differences as there are kinds of sciences and arts, and in each science or art there are many kinds of principles, for concepts, definitions, axioms, and hypotheses in a science all differ from each other in kind, and similar remarks apply to art. So when Aristotle speaks of man's soul as being that which can know in a sense all things (431b20–1), perhaps he is including all the possible parts of the rational soul, not in the sense that there can be a person who would ever know all things, for time does not allow this, but in the sense that, under certain circumstances, any given thing can be known by some person, for the rational power in its entirety includes that part which can acquire the knowledge of that thing.

Evidently, progress in a science or an art or any field in which some rational power plays a part implies continual discovery or invention which must originate with some person, and sometimes with two or more persons independently of each other. Such contribution may be of greater or lesser importance; so, in a way, many contribute to progress, for some invent or discover things, others perfect them, still others draw conclusions, and so on. But, when we speak of great originality or talent or a natural gift, usually we mean a rational power whose fulfillment results in a great contribution.

One might wonder how a natural gift of a person, whether an artist or a scientist, produces great works of art or discovers great truths. Observation of human activities hardly gives us a clue. Such a person seems to tread on familiar grounds or swim in familiar waters, so to speak, as if he or she had been there before and knows where to go and what to do, like birds which go south for the winter but north for the summer. Perhaps there is an affinity or kinship between a natural gift as a power and the objects to which that power is directed, like the power to see and the objects of vision. Thus gifted poets seem to have an intuitive sense—an intuition or intellect in Aristotle's way of speaking (99b20–100b19)—of what fits well and what does not. When they introduce a phrase in the making of a poem and reflect on it, they sense intuitively that the phrase fits well, or that it should be replaced. Similarly, a gifted scientist seems to know what questions to ask and what means to use in solving a scientific problem. We often speak of an acquired habit as being a second nature to us, for it is stable and functions without much effort. Then one's first nature, which is a form or a set of powers, would be more stable and superior to that habit; for such are the powers of seeing and hearing and the others, in fact, such is one's very nature. A natural gift, then, being no part of rationality which is common to the human species but being something added to the common part like a dividend at birth, would appear to lie between the common part of rationality and one's acquired habits; for habits may change by intention or lack of use and are often directed by thought, but a natural gift is rather independent and less subject to such change and seems to be more stable than a habit because, being inherited, it is closer to the common part of rationality.

To try to analyze a natural gift presupposes that an analysis is possible, and to seek some cause of its nature presupposes that there is such cause. If neither a cause can be found nor an analysis made, should one then consider it to be a principle? But a principle tends to be simple and uncaused and the starting point of other things, whereas a natural gift is observed to be directed to many and various objects, as is general prudence, which in a sense is all–inclusive in direction and one of the greatest gifts of man in practical affairs

(1144b32–1145a9). On the other hand, the simplicity of a principle does not prevent it from being applied or directed to many different things, like the principle "Action and reaction are equal and opposite," whose application is pervasive, or the principle "Sums of equals are equal," which is applicable to lines, planes, numbers, and many other things. Vision, too, is a simple power and a principle, yet it enables us to see a great variety of things. If so, perhaps a natural gift, too, is a principle, and also simple, and capable of being directed to many and different things coming under a genus.

We have stated, then, that a work of art may be produced either by art (when one learns from others) or by the artist's special nature in the manner we have indicated. So since a work of art cannot be produced in any other way, we may lay down the following definition of an artist, which is more inclusive than the provisional one given previously.

> DEF: An artist is a person who can produce works of art by art or by a natural gift.

Whether Aristotle used a Greek term for "artist" or some other term for a person with a gift is not clear, but he was aware of the distinctions as we have stated them. In either case, it makes little difference, for what is important is perceiving and making distinctions rather than attaching names.

Evidently, both the artists who possess the gift and those without the gift must use true reason which is individual and do so knowingly, for both must identify and deal with individual things correctly to produce works of art. But the artists without the gift must use rules or true reason which is general and has been gained mainly through instruction from others. The artists with the gift need instruction less than do the artists without the gift, for they proceed intuitively and usually *in accord with* true reason more than *with* true reason. Further, production *with* rather than *in accord with* true reason which is general happens to belong to the artists without the gift more than to the artists with the gift. The former artists know the rules and usually the true reasons because they have received them from their instructors explicitly, whereas the latter artists are directed intuitively by their gifts more than by explicitly stated true reasons.

Perhaps it is partly because of what has just been said that, more often than not, artists with the gift are superior to artists without the gift when it comes to teaching gifted students but inferior to them in teaching students without the gift. For students without the gift are more in need of explicitly stated instructions than students with the gift, whereas gifted students learn more by observing and imitating productions intuitively than by reading or listening to statements, and it is the teacher with the gift who excels in displaying production by acting intuitively. There is another reason: unlike artists without the gift, gifted artists tend to be somewhat impatient with average students and are not much interested in learning the art of teaching such students. This happens with teachers of science also. Clearly, then, gifted artists who proceed mainly *with* true reason which is both general and individual are rare in literature and fields in which productions of works of art do not require much logical and technical knowledge, such as mathematics or physics. Besides, the subject matter in their fields does not lend itself to the kind of accuracy which exists in some of the natural sciences, and such artists, if they happen to ponder whether scientific or general knowledge would be of use at all, will often, if not usually, avoid the effort of acquiring such knowledge; for they may conclude that the gains will not be worth the effort, or that they have no scientific bent, or that science and art do not mix, etc. But artists who need technique and advanced knowledge in the natural sciences to produce works of art are not as rare, for suspension bridges, airplanes, satellites, and other such artistic works must be produced with advanced knowledge of mathematics and physics and other such sciences, and such knowledge, which is general, is usually acquired *with* reason.

The solution to the other problem, i.e., whether a person can be a great artist without learning from others the needed scientific truths according to which works of art are produced, follows as a corollary from what has been said so far. We stated that human nature includes the power to acquire and use reason, that some persons may also have inherited a natural gift in a special field, such as music or literature, that they cannot produce a work of art unless they act *in accord with* some general truths concerning that work, and that they may use their gift to act *in accord with* true reason which is general and still not act *with* that reason, i.e., knowingly. It follows, then, that a work of art in a field which does not require for its production much advanced technical and scientific knowledge may be produced by an artist whose gift, as it matures, becomes strong enough to produce that work, not so much *with* true reason which is general, but rather *in accord with* that reason or the corresponding rules. A gifted artist, however, who produces a work of art also *with* true reason which is general in such a field is a rarity.

Let us now consider briefly the nature of application and see how attributes of individuals, whether works of art or not, can be investigated by science. Application, like perception, comes under the category of relation; and just as there are two parts in perception, i.e., that which perceives and that which is perceived, so there are two parts in application, that which is applied and that to which something is applied. Now application has many senses, but here it will be considered only to the extent needed in our discussion of art and of applied science. A strict scientific treatment of application need not be given here, but an informal description along with examples would be sufficient for our purpose.

It can be shown that a theorem is general in the highest degree, and that, if "every A is B" is a theorem, B belongs to A through the cause but does not so belong to any other thing. If, on the other hand, B belongs to other things besides A, the statement "every A is B" is not a theorem, for it is not general enough, but let it be called "an application." The word "belong," it may be added, has two meanings: (a) in "every man is an animal" the term "animal" is predicated of every man, but (b) in "every triangle has angles," angles are present in a triangle, for one cannot truly say that every triangle *is* angles. Aristotle's meaning of "belonging" is as follows: B is said to belong to A if it is either a predicate of A or present in A. An application, then, is a statement which is not a theorem and in which that which belongs to a subject belongs also to other subjects.

The statement "gold sinks in water," although general, is an application, for sinking in water is also an attribute of other things besides gold, and hence "sinking in water" is predicable of and also applicable to "gold" or gold, to "silver" or silver, etc. Similarly, "tragedy is a poem" is an application for a similar reason; hence "a poem" is both predicable of and applicable to "tragedy" or tragedy, to "comedy" or comedy, etc. Each of these applications is a part of a science, the first being a part of physics, the second being a part of the science whose subject is the art of poetry, and let such applications be called "corollaries."

Again when a man thinks truly that a given piece of metal is gold, he applies his concept "gold" to that individual metal; and when a poet,

in producing a given tragedy, introduces as the tragic hero someone
who is better than an average person but who makes an error unknowingly, he or she applies to the hero so chosen the thought that a choice
of a man with such disposition is better for a tragedy than a choice of
someone who is inferior to an average man. In both these examples,
one applies a thought or an expression which is general to an individual, and such application is not a part of a science, since the subject is
an individual.

It is evident from the definitions that a corollary is an application,
but that an application is not necessarily a corollary. For, whereas a
corollary may be a part of a science and may be used directly as a
premise in discovering theorems in that science, an application whose
subject is an individual cannot be a part of a science but may be used
in discovering attributes of an individual *with the aid of a science*. For
example, if we perceive that the moon is a body whose shape is spher-
ical, knowledge of the properties of a body from physics and of a
sphere from mathematics enables us to know that these are attributes
(but not properties) of the moon. Again, ability to learn grammar is a
property of humans but an attribute and not a property of an individual. Similarly, one can best evaluate or construct a good tragedy or
comedy or imitative work of literature, which is an individual, if one
has the skill and proceeds *in accord with* the truths used by the corresponding art; and such truths are parts of the corresponding productive science. In general, then, knowledge of the attributes of an
individual, whether with respect to truth or beauty or goodness, depends partly on application, partly on scientific knowledge, and
partly on ability to discover truths or skill to produce works of art. We
have stated and illustrated, then, the method which Aristotle regards
as the means by which knowledge of individuals can be obtained with
the aid of science or used to produce works of art.

It would appear that a thing produced by art may be a substance or
an attribute of (or in) a substance; for a house and a chair as products
of art are thought to be artistic substances, but the health produced in
person by the doctor is an attribute, and so are the kinds of motions of
the dancers, for they have been caused partly by the instructor's art.
On the other hand, a production is a generation, and the underlying
subject (often called "matter" or "material cause") during the process
of generation is acquiring something, whether a form or something
else, and what results at the end of the generation appears to be al-

ways a composite of matter and form and not just an attribute. The problem which arises here, namely, whether what is produced must be a composite of matter and form or not, may be resolved by a discussion of generation, and by "generation" here we mean essential generation, which is a change of or in a material subject.

In any generation, that which is generated is generated *by something*, and *out of something*, and *becomes something* at the end of the generation (224a21–5b9). The two essential kinds of generation are that *by nature* and that *by art*, in which nature and art are the two *moving causes*, respectively, for each of them initiates the generation (1032a12–3a23). That out of which a thing is generated is the underlying subject, and that which results at the end of the generation is a work of nature if the moving cause is nature, but usually a work of art if the moving cause is art. The difference is illustrated in an oak tree generated from an acorn in the first case and a statue by a sculptor in the second case. At the end of the generation, the underlying subject may either assume a new form, or keep the same form as before but change with respect to an attribute. For example, the acorn which becomes an oak tree changes with respect to form, but a person who becomes taller does not change in form but changes with respect to height, which is a quantity and so an attribute. Now an unqualified generation is defined as a change of a material thing with respect to its form, but a qualified generation is defined as a change of a material thing with respect to an attribute of it and not with respect to its form.

From the two examples of generation just given and the two definitions posited, it is evident that, of essential generations by nature, some are unqualified and some are qualified.

Since, by definition, a production according to Aristotle is a generation by art, a production too would be either unqualified or qualified. Thus, an industrial chemist as an artist can use elements or compounds to produce such compounds as are also generated or exist by nature; so from certain composite substances one can produce substances which are composites with different forms, and such productions are evidently unqualified. For example, water can be produced both by nature and by art from oxygen and hydrogen. A person who is cured by a doctor and gains health, on the other hand, does not change with respect to form at the end of that change. The change from disease to health by a doctor is a change with respect to an attribute, and so the production is qualified.

But there is a problem in the case of certain works of art, e.g., statues and houses and chairs, which are regarded as artistic substances. Should the shapes of these be called "forms" in the same sense as the natural forms, such as those of animals or of plants? If all artistic substances are to be regarded as substances, then just as the generation of an oak tree from an acorn is unqualified, so the generation of a house from its materials would be unqualified. But is the shape of the statue of a person the same as the form of that person?

The form of a woman is her soul (412a19–21), but the shape of the statue, which is said to imitate her, is an imitation not of her soul but of one of her attributes, namely, of her outward shape. So, in saying that the statue is a composite with shape as its form and bronze as its matter, one would be using the word "form" not in the same sense as that which it has in natural substances. In fact, such form, being a surface and so a quantity, is an imitation of an attribute of a person. Consequently, the statue itself, if it is to be called "a substance," should be regarded as inferior to a natural substance, for its so–called "form" is an attribute. Moreover, when scientists investigate the bronze's nature, which is the form of bronze, they pay no attention to the shape of the bronze but regard shape as an accident and not as the form of it. What they seek is a set of essential elements or attributes which, taken together, will enable them to define or identify bronze regardless of its shape.

Again, the form of a natural thing, whether animate or inanimate, requires the kind of matter which is proximate and hence proper to that form and which makes possible the thing's behavior. For example, a human soul, which is proper to man, requires the kind of matter—i.e., flesh and bones and the like—which enables a person to sense, think, move from place to place, and perform other such functions. The matter of the statue of a person, on the other hand, need not have such specific requirements, unless one wishes to go as far as to assert that solidity, which is an attribute of the matter of bronze and of iron and of wood and of a host of other things differing in nature or kind, should be added, in which case solid matter would be the matter of the statue. Even so, solid matter, being general and not proximate or specific, differs from flesh and bones and the like, which are specific, for it could be the matter of a saw and a house and many other things also.

It is in view of the above remarks that Plato, according to Aristotle

(1070a18–21), in positing the Ideas (or Forms) as being eternal, the most real, separate from each other and from other things, and the causes of all those things, did not include Ideas of beds and statues and other artistic works of this sort. He regarded all natural things as imitations of the corresponding Ideas and less real than those Ideas; and since works of art for him were imitations of natural things, he regarded such works as being less real than even natural things and inferior to them.

It appears, then, that works of art which cannot be works generated by nature are, if at all, substances in a secondary sense.

What is imitation according to Aristotle? By "imitation" here we mean artistic imitation, i.e., a work of art, the kind which requires art to be produced; and we shall use that term to include in its meaning, besides the work of art as such, also what that work is a sign of. No definition of such imitation appears in Aristotle's extant works. However, from a list of the things to which Aristotle applies the term in the *Poetics*, we may get some idea of his meaning, and, by induction, we shall try to frame a definition which is at least consistent with what he says in that work.

Let us assume that an artist, A, has used art, B, to produce a work of art, C, which imitates an object, D. The word "imitation" as a relative term is similar to the word "teacher," which is a relative term also; for just as we speak of a teacher as a person who is related to another person—a student—by imparting knowledge to the latter, so we speak of an imitation as being a work of art which is related to the object imitated by standing for or portraying that object. There are other meanings of "imitation," but they need not be considered here. The inquiry into the nature of C and of D here is an inquiry into the manner in which C as an imitation is related to D as the object imitated.

Now C may be either in the mind of the artist or not in that mind, and it may be either an individual or in some way universal; and the same may be said of D. For example, if a painter produces a painting of an actual tree, the painting as a work of art is an individual existing not in the painter's mind but outside of it, and what is imitated is itself an individual existing not in the painter's mind. But if a composer creates a tune without putting it on paper, the tune exists in the composer's mind, not as an actual tune but as a thought of that tune; and if that thought is put on paper, what exists on paper is still not a tune but a symbol of a tune. So in both cases the work of art is a symbol of the tune and not the tune itself. Further, just as the word "circle" signifies a circle universally taken and not an individual circle, so both the thought of the tune and the writing of it are symbols of the tune *as if taken universally*; for it is only when the tune is actually played that we have individual instances of the tune as a work of art, although not the same work of art as it exists in the composer's mind or on paper. Moreover, the tune can be played many times and by many, usually with different interpretations by different performers. Here it is really the art of the performer as a performer which causes the performance of the actual tune as an individual, whereas the tune as it exists in the mind of the composer or on paper functions *as if it were a universal*; and as such it is somewhat analogous to the term "circle," which is universal. We have shown in the two examples just given, then, that C as a relative may be taken either as an individual or universally, as it were, and either external to the mind or in the mind of the producer; and the same may be said of D. These facts and other statements in the *Poetics* suggest a definition of an artistic imitation, and, in particular, of one which exists in poems, as in a tragedy.

> DEF: An artistic imitation, whether in the mind or external to the mind, is a work of art which stands for or portrays any one of the following: an object (1) as it is or was, or (2) as it should be, or (3) ideally, or (4) with respect to its nature or universality, whether according to probability or necessity, or (5) as it is thought or said to be or to have been according to (1) or (2) or (3) or (4).

The above definition appears to include the kinds of objects which Aristotle advocates as being, or allows to be, objects of imitation in the construction of a good tragedy. Thus, according to lines 1460b22–26 of the *Poetics*, certain kinds of impossibilities would be allowed as objects of imitation, and since by definition an object includes impossibilities, the term "object" in the definition of artistic imitation would allow some impossibilities under certain circumstances. Of the things which may be imitated, those coming under (a) and (b) in line 1460b10 of the translation are included in the parts (1) and (5) of the definition of artistic imitation, those coming under (c) in line 1460b11 are included in parts (2) and (3), and those coming under the modality of things (i.e., necessity, probability, universality) as stated in Section 9 of the *Poetics* are included in part (4). Evidently, the definition of imitation just given is consistent with all the kinds of imitation which, according to Aristotle, may or should be used in a tragedy or an epic.

Some works of art are simple, and many of them of the same kind may be produced by a single artist, as in the case of shoes or chairs or statues. In some cases, the same artist may produce works of many species under a genus, as in the case of a composer who can produce sonatas and symphonies and other species of music, and in the case of a musical artist who can play a number of instruments. There are also works of art whose complexity requires the work of many kinds of artists under the direction of a master artist, e.g., the master architect of the Woolworth Building or the conductor of an orchestra. In rare cases, a work of art requires arts in many genera or fields, as in the case of planning a new town or city.

Can an art be a work of art, or conversely? Typical examples of art are engineering, carpentry, sculpture, medicine, and gymnastics, and the corresponding works of art are bridges, tables, statues, health, and physical fitness in a person. These examples suggest that an art differs from the corresponding work of art; for the art of the sculptor is not the statue, the art of the carpenter is not the table, and the same applies to the other examples. Art, we said, exists in the mind of the artist, but the corresponding works of art in these examples exist outside of the mind. Further, whenever the work of art exists in the mind, it can be shown that it exists not as an art but as something different from an art, as in the case of a student who is instructed in the art of teaching. If the teacher teaches the student verbally how to teach a subject, the student learns not the whole art of teaching but only a part of it, namely, general knowledge verbally of how to teach, because he or she learns from the teacher only the general truths or the corresponding rules of how to teach but has yet to acquire the skill of teaching students, and such skill takes a long time. So whether a work of art exists in the mind or outside of it, it cannot be an art since the corresponding skill will be missing. It is evident, then, that neither can art be a work of art, nor can a work of art be art; for, by logic, if A cannot be B, neither can B be A.

Can an art be a science, or conversely? If an art were a science, since a science uses no skill but only general concepts and true reason which is general, an art would use no skill but only general concepts and true reason which is general. But this is impossible. Hence an art cannot be a science. One should not confuse skill, whose function is to participate in the production of works of art, which are individuals, with originality or ability to discover principles or demonstrate theorems, which are general. Conversely, a science is not an art, otherwise a science would require skill.

Now it appears that there is something common to a productive science and the corresponding art which uses that science, for, in both of them, use is made of the same true reason which is general. So one may be tempted to argue that an art includes or may include the corresponding science, as in the case of the medical art, which appears to include or use the truths of medical science. But, as indicated earlier, the function of a productive scientist differs from the function of the corresponding artist. The proper aim of that scientist as a scientist is primarily to discover principles and demonstrate theorems from those principles, all of which are general, and secondarily to acquire all these from others, whereas the proper aim of the artist as an artist is to produce works of art in accord with as much of the corresponding science as is needed, usually by *accepting* and *applying* the needed principles and theorems from the corresponding science without using demonstration, or else by using his or her natural gift. The fact that some artists are hardly articulate as to what principles or truths they use in production does not change the fact that, although they do not proceed *with* true reason which is general, they still can produce works of art *in accord with* such reason, whether with the aid of their gift or by the use of rules or both, as we have stated earlier. The function of artists as artists, then, does not include discovery of principles or demonstration of theorems, except perhaps occasionally; but if they do discover or demonstrate, they act as scientists and not as artists. Thus a scientist and the corresponding artist, when dealing with the same principles or truths, do so in different ways, and there is no duplication.

In general, then, the proper aim of a productive science as a science is limited primarily to the investigation and discovery of scientific principles and the demonstration of theorems from those principles, or else to acquire all these from others, whereas the proper aim of the corresponding art is the production of works of art with the aid of skill and in accord with the needed scientific principles and theorems. So, in one way, an art is related to the corresponding productive science by depending logically on that science for its concepts and truths, whether explicitly or implicitly, i.e., whether the works of art are produced *with* knowledge of the corresponding science used or *in accord with* that knowledge, for the function of an artist is not to discover those truths but to act in accord with them. In another way, a productive science is related to the corresponding art by depending on that art inductively, for the concepts and principles of that science are formed usually after the arts have advanced to some degree. For example, the art of tragedy existed before the first systematic science of tragedy, i.e., the *Poetics*, was written. What gives unity to a productive science and the corresponding art, however, is the proper end of art, namely, the work of art, or else the use or enjoyment of that work, if it is a final end, and in this sense, a productive science is instrumental to the corresponding art. This does not prevent the productive scientist or the artist from enjoying as such his proper activity.

It happens sometimes that the same problem requires for its solution the aid of both the scientist and the artist. For example, the problem of discovering the speed of light belongs to mathematical physics, but the construction of the proper instruments to be used for that discovery belongs to the corresponding art. Sometimes the same person plays both roles; for example, some medical discoveries were made by physicians and not by medical scientists. One may add: other things being equal, an artist who possesses also the corresponding productive science has an advantage over an artist without that science, and if the artist is also gifted, especially in both the art and the corresponding science, he or she has the strongest unity and excels all others in the field of that art.

PART IV: *AIMS OF ART*

It was stated in Part II that the unity of a science may be specified by one subject, which may be either one genus of things or one aim (1003a33–b15). These two general types of unity arise in view of the fact that (a) scientific knowledge is a relation of the knower to the known (6a36–b6), and the fact that (b) there are many kinds of aims which cause the different activities of knowers and also many kinds of knowable things which may be investigated. In one way, then, there can be as many kinds of sciences as there are kinds of scientifically knowable things; in another, there can be as many kinds of sciences as there are kinds of activities chosen by the scientists. A theoretical scientist as a scientist chooses activities for their own sake, a productive or a practical scientist as a scientist, on the other hand, chooses activities for some other end. So one principle according to which unities in the sciences arise is the kind of activities with respect to an end, another is the kind of things which are scientifically knowable.

When we compare the artist with the scientist we discern both similarities and differences. Let the term "discovery" for the moment mean discovery of scientific principles and of demonstrations of theorems. Then production is to the artist as discovery is to the scientist; the thing produced is to the artist as the thing discovered is to the scientist. Both production and discovery are in some sense relations, the first being a relation of the artist's activity to the work of art which is being produced, the second being a relation of the activity of the scientist to the scientifically knowable. Further, like a scientist, an artist may produce a work of art not for the sake of the proper end of that work but for some other end. For example, a car manufacturer may choose profit rather than good quality as his primary aim, and a composer may cater to the common people for popularity as well as for profit.

On the other hand, a work of art exists usually outside of the mind and only occasionally in the mind, as shown earlier, whereas a thing discovered or learned in a science, being a principle or a demonstration of a theorem and hence general knowledge, can exist primarily only in the mind of the scientist. Another essential difference is the fact that the activity of the scientist may be an end in itself, as in the case of theoretical or practical activity, or a means to another end, as in the case of the activity of a productive scientist as a scientist, whereas the activity of the artist appears to be limited to production, which is always a means to another end, i.e., to a work of art. One may argue that a carpenter may enjoy producing chairs and hence that such activity may be enjoyable and so an end in itself, although it results in the production of chairs, which are essentially instrumental and not ends in themselves. Yet one may wonder whether the carpenter would still enjoy that activity if told that the chairs would be destroyed immediately when completed. Is not his enjoyment due to his anticipation of the product or its effect, which will be caused by him and be regarded with pride as if his own for a period of time, like a baby brought into existence by its parents? It appears, then, that the activity of the carpenter may or may not be enjoyable; consequently, enjoyment would not be essential to the production of a chair but an accident of that production in the manner stated.

Further, a work of art, although being the proper end of the activity of an artist, is not an end in itself but a means to another end. For example, the proper end of a composer is the music composed, but for the audience (and even the composer) it is the effect of that music when played—i.e., the enjoyment of it—and not the music itself that is the final end (i.e., an end in itself which by its nature is pleasant). The same applies to paintings and novels and other such works of art, which are usually called "fine arts." Steel, too, which is the end of steel–making, is not a final end, for we are not affected pleasantly by steel as such; it is a means to still another end, e.g., to spoons and forks, which in turn are not final ends but means to other ends, e.g., to their use by man, if final ends, but for sale, if means to still other ends. The same applies to cloth and leather and other such works of art, which are usually called "useful arts."

It is evident from these and other such examples that, in the case of fine works of art, it is neither the activity of the artist that is the proper final end, although that activity may be enjoyable, nor the work produced, but the effect of that work on the spectators; in the case of useful works of art, on the other hand, even the effect of the work produced may not be the proper final end, as in the case of the effect of steel in the example given, so we must go for the proper final end to the effect of a later work produced from steel, e.g., to the use of spoons in the same example. In general, then, the proper final end of an artist's activity is or may be at least twice removed from that activity. In the case of fine works of art, the final end of the artist's activity is twice removed from that activity; for example, one interval is from the composer's activity to the music composed, the other, from the music composed to its effect, which is the enjoyment of music. In the useful arts, the final end may be even further removed from the activity of the artist; for example, in the case of spoons we may have three intervals: from the steel–maker's activity to steel, from steel to spoons, and from spoons to their use, their final end, if spoons are not used for sale or for some other things.

The term "art" in the expressions "fine art" and "useful art," we may add, signifies literally not art as defined earlier but a work of art, which is one of the meanings of "art" according to English dictionaries; for art as defined earlier is an ability of a certain kind, and it is not art as an ability that may be fine or give us pleasure but a work of art. Abilities as such are qualities (9a14–27), but pleasure in us arises when a fine work of art affects, not art as an ability, but vision or hearing or some other power when that power is in a state of awareness and is being moved by a mover, which is the object that causes enjoyment or pleasure.

But there is a problem. We enjoy also the effects of such works of art as bread, cheese, and warm clothing during the winter. Should these works, too, be called "fine works of art?" Is there a third kind of works of art besides the fine and the useful or should those works be called "useful?"

Perhaps the distinction between fine works of art (or works of fine art, if you wish) and the other works of art may be clarified by reference to two principles which Aristotle uses to distinguish the aims of men. He uses the terms "living" and "living well" as those principles (656a3–8). Living well for man is the same as or a property of living happily, and the good life is the same as or a property of happiness or a happy life. A person who pursues as final ends only the effects of material goods or the pleasures of the senses indiscriminately cannot be truly said to live well but just to live, even if he succeeds in his pursuit and leads a contented life. Such life hardly differs from that of the other animals, whose pleasures are limited to those of the senses and whose life can at best be one of contentment, which is similar or analogous to the life of a contented pet. So, in the case of some works of art which are not fine, as in those which are fine, the activity of the artist is twice removed from the final end. Happiness, however, is not just contentment but includes also the use of true reason in activities which are concerned with worthy and noble objects; for the human race is distinguished from the other animals by having reason, and the best end of humans is the best use of reason *in all* their activities, with emphasis on those which are of great importance. This end is usually called "happiness," and Aristotle defines happiness as the activity of the soul according to complete virtue (1102a5–6).

Such being the aim of a person, its fulfillment is attainable only by the use of the virtues, i.e., the acquired habits which dispose one to be engaged in activities as final ends in accord with the best use of true reason. This fact can be shown also by the following argument. Nature does nothing in vain but always tends to act for the best (271a33). A thing by nature—and a person as a composite of matter and form is a thing by nature—acts for the best if it uses the best that is proper to it (192b8–16, 704b12–17). That which is proper to a person is reason, and the best use of reason is the activity in accord with true reason for noble things. If stability is added to that activity, it becomes an activity in accord with complete virtue, i.e., it becomes happiness at its best. It is evident, then, that a happy life includes as a part contentment in accord with true reason, for contentment excludes pain, but that a contented life is not necessarily a happy life, for it may be a life in accord with true reason but not in accord with complete virtue.

A contented life as such, it may be repeated, may exist in humans as well as in animals, and the things with which such life is concerned are food, shelter, procreation, and the like, all of which are called "necessities of life." But the manner in which such life is realized by humans differs from that in which it is realized by the other animals, which have no reason at all, whether true or false. Since rationality is the differentia of humans, reason usually permeates all of human activities, including those which are concerned with the necessities of life. Yet even if activities concerned with such necessities excel in being performed in accord with true reason, they hardly compare with some other activities which are highly regarded and which are noble or contribute to the happiness of mankind. We bestow great honors on great public figures and great composers and great scientists, but we are not similarly disposed to honor an epicure or an elegant dresser or a great lover. The activities of the latter may be concerned mainly with the necessities of their own life rather than with what is regarded as noble and as contributing to their good life or also to that of others.

The solution to the problem concerning the enjoyment of such works of art as cheese and bread and the like is now evident from what has been said. Such enjoyment may be a final end for a life which aims only at contentment. If pursued as a part of happiness in accord with true reason, however, happiness is enhanced, but if pursued not as a part of happiness or even indiscriminately, happiness is certainly marred, whether directly or indirectly, for such a state of affairs disturbs the richness and harmony of virtuous activities and hence the happy life itself.

PART V: *ART AND THE POETICS*

We may now turn to poetics as Aristotle conceived it in writing the *Poetics*. First, using the definitions and distinctions already made, we must inquire logically whether poetics is a science or an art or a work of art or a theory or literary criticism. Having done this, we should then proceed to discuss and frame a definition of poetics. Finally, we must state its proper aim and inquire if it also has some other aim, for ends according to Aristotle may be proper or final or accidental or contributory or ultimate.

We should also keep in mind that the Greek terms whose usual translations are "poem," "poetry," "poetics" and other cognates do not have exactly the same meanings as they do for us and that, due to the lack of equivalent English terms, we have kept these traditional translations but have specified what their meanings will be, thus lessening the likelihood of verbal arguments, disagreements, and unfair criticism.

What is the genus of poetics? Is poetics a work of art? But a work of art, whether a substance or an attribute, is something individual produced by an artist who has used, directly or indirectly by means of rules or by his or her gift, true reason, both general and individual. All essential statements in the *Poetics*, on the other hand, are general, and statements which appear in that work about individuals have been introduced as illustrations or to confirm general truths but are not essential parts of that work. Further, if a work of art is useful (i.e., instrumental), like a house or a knife or a car, we speak of it as being comfortable or efficient or profitable, and if it comes under what one usually calls "fine arts," we speak of it as being beautiful or aesthetic or something of this sort. But these adjectives do not apply to the *Poetics*, for this work is concerned with the nature of a good poem and the manner in which it can be produced, so to regard the style of the *Poetics* as being prosaic, commonplace, cramped, lacking beauty or other literary embellishments is to misapprehend its function. Again, if one were to assert that the *Poetics* itself is an individual work produced by Aristotle and is therefore a work of art, the term "produced" would be misused. Further, every book on mathematics or chemistry or any science in general would likewise have to be a work of art and not a work on science, contrary to the definition of a science as defined and usually accepted. Again, if one were to assert that there is truth not only in the sciences but also in good poems, which we call "fine works of art," we would be using the term "truth" metaphorically and not scientifically. Metaphorical truth has no place in the sciences, and if there is any literal truth in such poems, it is not investigated or discussed scientifically but only used for some other purpose. It is evident from these arguments, then, that the *Poetics* or poetics in general is not a work of art.

Is poetics an art? But an art includes skill, and skill can exist only in the mind; hence art itself must exist only in the mind. Poetics, however, can also exist outside of the mind, i.e., as something written or printed or put in some other symbolic form, like Aristotle's *Poetics*. Besides, one who has an art can produce many works of that art, whereas one who has memorized and understands poetics or the *Poetics* of Aristotle may have no skill to produce works of art. Consequently, the *Poetics* or poetics in general is not an art.

Is poetics a theory? A theory, whether consisting of one or more hypotheses along with the conclusions which follow, or being a part of a science, like the theory of equations or of evolution or the Big Bang theory of the universe, would in each case come under a science or be itself a science; so this question need not be considered if the question "Is poetics a science?" is considered.

Is poetics literary criticism? The main definition of literary criticism appears to be: analysis and judgment of literary works of art. Let this be assumed. To make a good critical analysis of a literary work, then, would be to analyze well that work into its qualitative and quantitative parts and to judge them truly with respect to their merits. We may add, since one may err in analyzing well or judging truly a literary work of art, let the contrary of "good critic" be "bad critic."

There are two ways in which one may be said to be a good literary critic: (1) if one can analyze well and judge truly in a systematic way literary works of art of a certain kind (e.g., tragedies in general), or (2) if one is engaged in analyzing well and judging truly individual works of art of a certain kind as wholes with parts. A good literary critic in sense (2) presupposes a good literary critic in sense (1), whether directly or indirectly. We add the word "indirectly" because one who has a strong gift or knows the rules to analyze well and judge truly need not have formal knowledge of (1). Evidently, the *Poetics* is not literary criticism in sense (2), for it neither analyzes nor judges any individual work of art in its entirety; it tries to analyze well and judge truly in sense (1) tragedy and epic as wholes along with their parts *in general*. The *Poetics*, then, might be regarded, if at all, as literary criticism in sense (1), and so might poetics in general.

Now literary criticism in sense (1) contains expressions of the form "such and such is the case" or "such a part must have such attributes to be good" or "such a thing has such effect on the listener" or the like (1151a36–b11), each of which is a general statement and must therefore be either true or false. Since this kind of criticism contains essentially only general statements, it follows that good literary criticism in sense (1) which includes also axioms and definitions and hypotheses would not be different from a science. Further, since such criticism is concerned with how good works of art can be produced, it would not differ from a productive science, for both would be concerned systematically and in the same way with the same subject, namely, how best to produce certain literary works of art. In short, the *Poetics* or poetics in general is a productive science, and "productive science" is a genus of poetics, although not the proximate genus; for "productive science of the art of fine works," too, is a genus of poetics, in fact, a more proximate genus of poetics than is the genus "productive science."

In matters of art one should distinguish (a) the productive science, (b) the corresponding art, and (c) the works produced by that art. In literature, for example, there are poetics, the art of poetry, and poems. Poetics is a productive science, and its subject is the art of poetry; the art of poetry is the skill capable of producing poems in accord with true reason, both general and individual, and when in activity, that art (or the artist) is acting as the moving cause of the poems which are being produced; and the poems are the works produced by the art of poetry (or by the poet). Now the term "poetics" is a genus, and so is the expression "the art of poetry" and also the term "poem." One species of poems is "tragedy"; the corresponding art may be called "art of tragedy" or "tragic art"; and the corresponding science may be called "the science of tragic art" or "the science of how to produce good tragedies." Similar remarks apply to the species "comedy," "dithyramb," "flute–playing," to each of the rest species of works of the poetic art, and also to their corresponding arts and sciences.

It is evident from the first sentence of the *Poetics* that all the species of things which have been translated as "poems" have something in common: the plot, which has a beginning and a middle and an end. So since a poem, unlike a painting or a statue, cannot as a whole be grasped at a glance but takes time to be read or performed or in general perceived, the works coming under the poetic art do not include statues or paintings or other such static works, although these, too, are forms of imitation (1448b4–12, 1454b8–10, 1460b7–11). Further, there are other forms of literature which, although called "poems" nowadays, do not come under the genus *"poiema,"* which is usually translated as "poem" for lack of a better English word. Consequently, in examining the *Poetics*, a critic should limit his judgment to what Aristotle states he is about to discuss and not criticize the *Poetics* unfairly, as some do, by saying that Aristotle's concept of a poem is narrow because it fails to include other forms of poems or literature for consideration. Such a critic might as well criticize a mathematician for not including also physics and chemistry in his discussion of mathematics. Aristotle was well aware of such works of literature as speeches, addresses, orations, prayers, and others which have no plots and hence are not poems in the sense in which he defined what is usually translated as "poems." Whether he discussed any of the other forms systematically in other works is entirely a different matter.

Let us turn to poetics and frame a definition of it, basing our judgment on what is stated or implied in the *Poetics*. Poetics is a science, a productive science; its subject is the art of poetry; and this art is skill in accord with true reason in producing poems, each of which has a plot. In addition, the *Poetics* states that in tragedy the plot, which is as it were the soul of tragedy (1450a38), appears to be the primary part. Further, we were given the following list of kinds of poems, most if not all of which differ in species from each other: tragedy, epic, comedy, dithyramb, lyre–playing, flute–playing, syrinx–playing, and Panpipe–playing, with an indication in lines 1447a24–26 that there are still other species of poems. From all these and by the use of generalization, extrapolation, and other principles, some dialectical and others scientific, we may state the following definition of poetics:

> DEF: Poetics is a productive science whose subject, the art of poetry, is an art of making fine poems, each of which as a poem (1a) is an imitation having a plot as its primary and proper part, (2) differs in species from a poem of another species by using different means or imitating objects of a different kind or performing the imitation in a different manner, (3) uses rhythm or speech or harmony or some combination of these as materials, and (1b) ends in a catharsis of emotions proper to its species.

Let us now inquire whether poetics or poems in general aim at one final end or more than one. It was stated in Part II that the aim of a science may be proper or accidental. Since the accidents of a thing are indefinite and so indeterminate, there can be no science of them

(1026b2–15). Hence, in discussing poetics as a science, accidental aims or ends should be dismissed (1025a24–6, 1026b2–5).

But one aim or end may be related to another aim or end, respectively, as a part is related to a whole, in which case the aim or end of the part must also serve or be subordinated to the aim or end, respectively, of the whole. The proper end of one's eyes is to see visible objects well, that of ears is to hear audible sounds well, and the same applies to the end of each of the other bodily parts of man. Similarly, each of man's virtues (ethical or intellectual) has its own proper end. The proper end of a person as a whole, however, is happiness, which is a final end and also the ultimate end. But the proper end of each part (whether ethical or intellectual), if a final end, seems to be related to happiness as a part is to a whole. So if happiness is to be attained, each final end as a part, besides being enjoyable, must also serve a higher or more inclusive end, be it happiness or a final end which is less inclusive than happiness. Similar remarks apply to the associations of men. As Aristotle states in lines 1252a4–7 of the *Politics*, "while all associations aim at some good, the association which aims in the highest degree at the supreme good is the one which is the most authoritative and includes all the others. This association is called 'a state,' and it is a political association."

But there seems to be a difficulty. If happiness, which is a whole with parts, is attained when each part of it, being proper and final, is fulfilled, what need is there for a part to subserve happiness in addition to fulfilling its own function? It would appear that the fulfillment of each part, which is proper and final and hence enjoyable, will automatically lead to happiness if no other causes interfere. But the question raised may hide a logical flaw. If a thing is a man, then it is an animal, but if the thing is an animal, it is not necessarily a man. Similarly, one might argue that if there is to be happiness, each part of it must fulfill its proper end, which is final and enjoyable, but if each such part fulfills its proper end, it does not necessarily follow that the man will be happy. In other words, the proper and final end as a final end of each part when fulfilled is necessary but may not be sufficient for happiness; more is needed.

Let us take an example. The deliberate choice to listen to good rather than to bad music is a virtue, and such listening is enjoyable and so a final end and the proper effect of that music on the listener. But a man with a strong gift in some important field other than music may spend most of his daily life listening to good music and pay no attention to his inherited gift, or he may wish to develop his gift but avoid the effort of finding the right means to its development and its use. Does such avoidance to seek the right means assure him of happiness to the extent he is capable? What is needed is something additional: an overall intellectual virtue which, with the aid of perception of one's ultimate good (i.e., happiness) and the disposition towards it, will enable a person to deliberate well and find the means to attain the best that is possible by distributing his or her activities in the right proportion. Aristotle calls that overall ability "prudence"; and he uses the term "shrewdness" to mean the ability in general of finding any means, whether right or wrong, to attain any given end, whether good or bad (1144a1–5a11).

A prudent person, then, is one who has true perception of his or her or also of other persons' ultimate good, is disposed towards its attainment, and, if not impeded, is shrewd in achieving it, i.e., is able to deliberate well in finding the right means to happiness, whether his or her own or also that of others. An unscrupulous person, on the other hand, is one who perceives falsely what the ultimate human good is and is able and disposed to use successfully any means, right or wrong, to achieve a desired end; but that end, if fulfilled, usually goes against the person's own happiness because at least some of the activities as final ends will not be virtuous and will produce discord. In fact, the ethical virtues cannot be understood clearly or fulfilled properly without being emphasized correctly and directed by prudence, and this seems to be evident from the manner in which Aristotle defines ethical virtue; for virtue presupposes and requires (a) the perception of one's ultimate good and also (b) prudence to limit or direct or specify the function of each ethical virtue as a means to happiness to the extent possible. Now the perception of happiness and the possession of prudence may either be included in the definition of an ethical or intellectual virtue (except prudence), or else be stated as postulates of those virtues. If they are included, they need not be repeated whenever each specific virtue uses the genus "virtue" in its definition, for then every virtuous activity will be understood not separately from happiness but as a necessary part of happiness. In fact, Aristotle includes them for metaphysical reasons (1035b6–11, 1036b30–32). His definition of ethical virtue, for example, is as follows.

DEF: Ethical virtue is a habit, disposed towards *action* by deliberate choice, being the mean relative to us, and specified as a prudent man would specify it (1106b36–1107a2).

His argument is that a part is relative to the whole of which it is a part, depends on that whole for its existence and function, and must be defined in terms of that whole. For example, a hand may be defined as *a part* of a man who directs it to perform certain functions, whatever these may be. So since a given virtuous activity, viewed in this sense, becomes a part of happiness, and since happiness requires prudence among other things, a given virtuous activity, being a part of happiness, includes prudence as just defined and understood. For example, to be generous is not merely to give one's material goods to another, but to give the right amount, to the right person, in the right manner, for the right purpose, etc. Such donation requires for its proper fulfillment both knowledge and prudence, which are intellectual virtues (1106b14–24, 1138b15–34).

In short, if the proper end as a final end of each activity includes prudence in its definition to be rightly performed as a part of happiness, the fulfillment of such activity will be the best for happiness; but if that end does not include in its definition prudence, then happiness will not necessarily attain its maximum.

Now the contribution to happiness of man's enjoyment of poems cannot be understood apart from man's nature; after all, it is human and not divine happiness that we are considering. It was stated that man is a rational animal and is a composite of matter and form, of body and soul. Rationality as man's differentia, then, pervades all or almost all of man's activities, and it does so best if man's ultimate end is to be achieved according to human nature. But even if it does so best, not all kinds of best activities are of equal importance, whether one limits them to those which are pursued as final ends or not. Of those which are pursued as final ends, the primary are the theoretical, the practical, and also a third kind, for the enjoyment of poems is neither a theoretical nor a practical final end; and to activities of the third kind we may add the enjoyment in such activities as hobbies, listening to music, social gatherings, and others. Do activities of the third kind, besides being final ends, have a further function?

First, man is born without virtue or vice, for these are acquired habits, and at the first stage of life man can be content at best. Happiness would be best realized after one has gone through the stage of education and has acquired the virtues necessary for mature activity. During the stage of incompleteness, then, man would be in the process of being educated. Learning as a motion usually requires effort and is not without pain (1339a26–29); so the extent to which man can be partaking of happiness during this stage would be the degree to which man's virtuous activities, primarily the highest among the theoretical but secondarily those of *action*, have matured and have become independent. Consequently, one may truly speak of man at the early and learning stages as being content but not yet as being happy, except partly so, for complete happiness requires mature thinking.

During the mature and virtuous stage, and barring impediments, man would be happy either primarily, when engaged in theoretical activities, or secondarily, when engaged in virtuous *actions*, or else, when partaking of both kinds of activities (1177a12–78b35). But human happiness would require man to partake of both kinds of activities. For, as rational, one should be pursuing theoretical activities; as a material substance, one would need some ethical virtue to attend to the requirements of the body and of the necessities of life; and as a part of the state and not completely self–sufficient, one must use ethical virtue which is necessary in dealing with others. It appears, then, that a happy person must use both ethical and intellectual virtues. Also, the less one needs to attend to the necessities of life and to activities which require ethical virtue, the more one would be able to attend to theoretical activities, which are primary. Moreover, human happiness at its best could belong to him only during his mature years.

Being a composite of matter and form, however, man is subject to stresses and strains and to changes in general. In view of this, one's vocation, whether adopted by free choice or accepted by necessity, cannot always be pursued continuously for a long time but causes him to get tired; so one requires rest or relaxation (1176b32–5). During periods of rest, then, one usually chooses pleasant activities, which make him relax and return afresh to his vocational activity (1176b35–7a11). He may relax in two ways: (a) by himself, if, for example, he listens to music or enjoys reading a novel or is engaged in some hobby, or (b) with others, if, in general, he participates in enjoyable activities, such as gatherings, games, friendships, and other associations which bring men together. Activities which aim at useful works of art, being means to other ends, hardly contribute as such to an enjoyable relaxation, unless pursued as hobbies, like gardening. Relaxed activities, on the other hand, being pleasant and chosen as final ends, are needed regardless of one's vocation. It is evident, however, that persons whose vocation is limited to instrumental activities, especially those which deal with the necessities of life, are more in need of relaxation than are persons who pursue a life of *action*, and persons of *action* are more in need of relaxation than are those who pursue theoretical activity. Persons who are limited to instrumental activities, on the other hand, care more for profit and what is pleasurable to the senses than for virtue and what is noble, and, because of greater need and less education, they tend to choose for relaxation somewhat indiscriminately the pleasures of the senses more than the pleasures of the mind. Those who have chosen as a career the life of *action* require external goods and ethical virtue (i.e., mostly the virtues towards others) more than do those who pursue the theoretical life (1177a25–b31). In general, then, periods of rest or relaxation are necessary for all men, and they contribute to the happiness of those who are virtuous, but less so to those who are less virtuous.

Finally, how is the enjoyment of poems, which is a final end, related to man's ultimate end, which is happiness? Human happiness in the primary sense is theoretical activity, which is scientific activity and the use of the intellect, and the enjoyment of poetry, not being a scientific activity, does not come under such activity and hence not under theoretical activity or happiness in the primary sense. Nor does that enjoyment come under a practical or a productive activity. It would certainly be absurd to regard as happy one who spends most of his or her daily life listening to music or playing cards simply for enjoyment; he or she may be content, but not happy (1337b27–8a3). So since the enjoyment of poems is not a theoretical activity or a practical activity, nor any of the instrumental activities, whether serious or menial, it must be pursued during periods of rest, for pleasant activities are either serious or relaxed. This is also evident by induction, if one were to go over the various activities, and also from the way in which those of great virtue spend their time. So since periods of rest are more worthy of choice and relaxing and refreshing if virtuously pleasant than if without pleasure, and activities which are more refreshing animate people more and make those who pursue serious and noble activities more eager and sooner to return to them (for serious activities are more pleasant than relaxed activities to them

(1177a25–8b8)), it follows that the enjoyment of poems during periods of rest would contribute to the happiness of those who are virtuous, but indirectly. The enjoyment of good poems, then, although a final end and pleasant, functions also *in a way* for the sake of serious and noble activities which enhance happiness more than do relaxed activities (1176b34–7a6), for relaxed activities are limited mostly to the pleasure of the senses (1174b34–7a11).

But do poems, besides being enjoyable as final ends and contributing to happiness in the manner just stated, contribute to that happiness in some other way? It cannot be denied that a poem may be presented so vividly and effectively as to persuade someone who has doubts concerning the means to happiness to follow virtue rather than vice, knowledge rather than ignorance; but such effect would be an accident and not a part of the aim of a poem. If, however, a good poem can contribute to happiness in some other way, it would have to do so neither accidentally nor indirectly as already stated but through its nature. It might do this by enhancing one's happiness through the means to happiness, that is, by adding to or improving one's virtue, whether ethically or intellectually or in both ways. In fact, it can be shown that poems, at least some of them, can do this, but in a qualified way and usually during one's early years; for at the early stages of life one is incomplete in virtue, and good poems, besides being enjoyable, may by example direct a person's efforts towards virtue rather than vice. One who is already virtuous, however, would not be so affected. Accordingly, the effect of a good tragedy, to take an example, has to be related to the kind of audience: the same tragedy may have different effects on different kinds of spectators, for these may differ in ethical habits or maturity, in which case the effect of the tragedy with respect to its aim—its tragic pleasure—will differ.

Finally, one may raise the question, "Is the *Poetics* closely related in any way to morality or politics or rhetoric or religion or the state as these disciplines were understood in Aristotle's time?" For if it is, it is to one or more of these most of all that it would be so related. But, according to Aristotle, this question does not appear to differ in kind from the question, "Is mathematics closely related in any way to physics or to philosophy or to ethics?" It has been answered systematically in the *Posterior Analytics* and partly in the *Nicomachean Ethics*, the *Politics*, and the *Metaphysics* but may be considered briefly here.

For the sake of clarity, let us retain the terminology of Aristotle by using the term "ethics" instead of the term "morality" (or "science of morals") and the term "theology" instead of the term "religion." Aristotle sometimes uses the transliterated term "theologia" instead of the phrase which is usually translated as "metaphysics," and he would allow poems to serve the cause of popular religions, but only to the extent to which the virtues of such religions do not conflict seriously with the virtues which he advocates in his *Nicomachean Ethics* or *Politics*.

Now poetics, ethics, theology, politics, and the others as sciences have principles, of which some are common to all or to some of them but others are proper to each science; and all sciences as such must demonstrate theorems, i.e., prove conclusions through causes. Further, a theorem in one science cannot be a theorem in another science, as stated in Part II, for the premises used as a unit in the demonstration of each theorem in each science must be proper to that science, and no such unit of premises can be proper to another science (76a37–b22, 88a18–b8). Consequently, all the theorems of one science must be proper to that science, even if some of them which are used not as premises but as regulatory principles (such as the principles of logic) are common to all or to many sciences. It also follows that a property of a subject in a science cannot be a property of a subject in another science, but it may be an attribute and so predicable of or applicable to a subject in another science.

For example, poetic imitation is a property and an attribute of a poem in poetics but only an attribute of tragedy in the science of tragedy, and this is because there are also other species of poems which are poetic imitations. Pleasure is an attribute of happiness but not a property of it; for happiness also requires virtue, but pleasure may be caused also by vice. Again πr^2 as a measure of area is a property of the area of a plane circle in plane geometry but only an attribute of and so applicable to the surface of a round table in the science and the art of making tables.

It is evident from what has been said, then, that no theorem or property in poetics is a theorem or a property, respectively, in politics or in ethics or in any other science. If each science is to be in accord with its definition, it must investigate only those scientific truths which cannot be demonstrated by another science, even if one science is related to another as a genus to a species, e.g., as the science of triangles is related to the science of right triangles and as poetics is related to the science of tragedy. These consequences follow from the nature or formal cause of a science. Accordingly, how would it be possible for politics or ethics or rhetoric or any other science to influence or determine or have any effect on the demonstrations of theorems or properties in poetics with respect to the nature or formal cause of the subject of poetics? To say that the *Poetics* should be understood in the light or context of the political or religious or moral atmosphere in Aristotle's time would be contrary to Aristotle's concept of science and to many of his other views, and such opinions neither have been nor can be causally or analytically demonstrated, even by means of modern scientific thinking; for Aristotle's scientific method hardly differs from that of today. Poetics is independent of the other sciences with respect to the nature and properties of its subject, and the *Poetics* in particular must be judged neither psychologically nor by external accidents, but only by what it does and states.

The final cause of poetics, on the other hand, is not like the formal cause in this respect. For example, many sciences and their corresponding arts are used to produce a single house, but all of them, although differing in their proper functions or ends, have a single final end, namely, comfortable living in the house. Final causes are somewhat like proper ends; for just as one proper end may be subordinated to another proper end, so may one final cause to another final cause. The proper end of poetics is scientific knowledge of the nature of a good poem, the proper end of the art of poetry is the ability to make good poems; and the final end of both poetics and the poetic art is the enjoyment of seeing or reading a good poem. A detailed discussion of relations between final causes will not be undertaken here, but one important relation may be mentioned: the enjoyment of a poem according to Aristotle is a certain part of the ultimate final cause of man, i.e., it is a part of man's happiness and as such a part it is proper to periods of rest or relaxation.

GLOSSARY

The meaning of most key terms in the translation are made clear in the English-Greek Glossary by means of a definition or a property or a description or examples, and references are often given to the page and lines according to the Bekker text. If an English term is not always used in the same sense, its various meanings are listed and are separated by a semicolon or a period. A few terms appear sometimes in roman and sometimes in italic letters, but they usually differ in meaning. For example, the term "action" and "*action*" differ in meaning, and so do the terms "man" and "*man*." Synonyms are separated by a comma. Some English terms which have no corresponding terms in Greek are added in the Glossary to facilitate getting Aristotle's thought.

In the Greek-English Glossary, English synonyms used for the same Greek term which has a single meaning are separated by a comma; but if the English terms are separated by a semicolon or a period, they are not synonyms, and the different meanings of those terms are usually given in the English-Greek Glossary.

ability δύναμις A quality which can have an effect on something. Syn: "power."

absurd ἄτοπον

accident συμβεβηκός An attribute which belongs to a subject infrequently, or an event which occurs infrequently, for example, eight feet in height is an accident of a man, and so is finding a dollar when going to a grocery store; also, that which may or may not belong to a subject is said to be an accident.

accidentally κατὰ συμβεβηκός Syn: "indirectly."

according to κατὰ Syn: "in accord with," "with respect to," "in virtue of," "by virtue of" (73a27–b34, 1022a14–35).

accord with, in Same as "according to."

accurate ἀκριβής One discipline is more accurate than another if (a) the first includes the causes of the facts to a higher degree; or, if (b) the first is of the more abstract; or, if (c) the second contains additional principles (87a31–7, 982a25–8, 1078a9–13).

act, v. ποιεῖν

action ποίησις, ποιεῖν Syn: "production"; "any act" which need not signify a production.

action πρᾶξις An action limited to practical matters and chosen deliberately with certainty and without hesitation for its own sake or ultimately for the sake of something else in view. Syn: "doing," "deed."

activity ἐνέργεια A wide and indefinable term having such species as "*action*," "thinking," "awareness," "production," and the like. Syn: "actuality", "realization."

agent πράττων A character in a play represented by a performer or narrator.

agony περιωδυνία Extreme pain or distress.

ambiguous ἀμφίβολος Having two or more meanings. Syn: "equivocal."

analogy ἀναλογία Similarity of relation between two pairs; e.g., if A is to B as C is to D, then the first two terms in the order given are said to be analogous to the last two terms in the order given. A proportion is a special case of an analogy (74a17–25, 76a37–40, 98a20–23, 1457b16–22).

anapest ἀνάπαιστος A metrical foot of the form ˘˘¯, or xx/, that is, consisting of two short syllables followed by a long one, or two unaccented syllables followed by an accented syllable, respectively.

anger   ὀργή   A desire, accompanied by pain, to exact an apparent
  revenge because of what appears to be an unjustified belittling
  of what is due to a man or to those dear to him.
animal   ζῷον   Men are included.
animal (except man)   Same as "brute."
application   See Aristotle's Theory of Art, Part III.
archon   ἄρχων   One of the nine chief magistrates of ancient Athens.
aristocracy   ἀριστοκρατία   A government by the few who are virtuous.
art   τέχνη   An acquired skill which enables one to produce with
  true reason something which can be produced (1140a1–33).
art of poetry   See "poetic art."
art, poetic   See "poetic art."
art, work of   A work of art is that which is produced by an artist or his
  art, e.g., a chair, a poem, or a bridge.
attribute   πάθος   An attribute is usually a thing which belongs to a
  subject, but the subject does not belong to it. For example,
  weight belongs to a body, oddness belongs to a number, and
  voice belongs to a man.
bad   φαῦλος; πονηρός   Vicious; base.
barbarism   βαρβαρισμός   Syn: "jargon," "solecism."
beautiful   καλός
because   διὰ, διότι   In the sentence "A is C because of B," B is said
  to be the cause or *reason* why A is C. Syn: "through," "by
  means of," "by" (sometimes).
beginning   ἀρχή   Same as "principle."
behavior   A man's behavior includes his *actions*, sufferings,
  thoughts, productions and activities in general. Perhaps "per-
  sonality" comes close in meaning to behavior.
belief   ὑπόληψις   Its species are "scientific knowledge," "opinion,"
  "judgment," and others.
best   κράτιστος   The best tragedy is a species of the finest tragedy
  and is the kind in which the intended victim or the protagonist
  is recognized and the intended terrible deed is avoided.
body   σῶμα   Usually a physical body is meant.
brave   ἀνδρεῖος   Disposed to *act* nobly in dangerous situations.
  Syn: "manly."
brute   θηρίον   An animal, excluding man.
by   Same as "because" (sometimes).
by means of   Same as "because."

by nature φύσει

by virtue of Same as "according to."

can, v. δύνασθαι Be able to or capable of.

capability δύναμις Ability to act on a thing or be acted upon by a mover.

catharsis κάθαρσις Purification of emotions.

cause αἰτία, αἴτιον The reason why something exists or comes to be or is known (194b16–195b20, 1013a24–4a25). Syn: "*reason.*"

chance, n. αὐτόματον An accidental moving cause which is usually occasional or variable or indefinite (195b31–198a13).

chance τύχη A chance which is not caused or would not be caused by man's thought or deliberation.

change μεταβολή A generic term, its species being "generation," "destruction," "motion." The species of motion are "increase," "decrease," "alteration," and "locomotion."

character ἦθος; πράττων (a) In a man, his ethical qualities or habits, which are virtues or vices or a combination of these; (b) an agent in a play represented by a performer. Syn: "agent."

choral, adj. χορικός Sung by or recited by a chorus.

chorus χορός In Greek drama, a company of performers who embellished the play by singing or dancing or narrating with or without the performers.

city ἄστυ Usually, this was the seat of a state where the main government was located or functioned, the rest being the countryside or surroundings.

cogent χρηστός Credible, i.e., speaking and *acting* in a manner which reveals the speaker's intentions. 1454a16–20.

comedy κωμῳδία

common κοινός

common people δῆμος These include farmers, business men, those with some skill or trade, soldiers, seafarers, laborers, etc., as opposed to notables, refined, educated, statesmen, in short, the high classes of people (1291b17–30).

commos Same as "lamentation."

compassion φιλανθρωπία

competition ἀγών

complete τέλειος That of which no part is missing; that whose virtue or excellence within its genus cannot be exceeded, as a perfect doctor or flute player. Syn: "perfect." 1021b12–1022a3.

complication δέσις The part from the beginning of a tragedy until the last part after which a change from good fortune to misfortune occurs (1455b26–8).

congenital σύμφυτος Syn: "innate."

connective σύνδεσμος See lines 1456b38–57a6.

consistent ὁμαλός Speaking or *acting* in accord with one's character.

consistent Statements or *thoughts* which do not imply contradiction.

contentment Pleasure throughout life without the use of virtue. See Aristotle's Theory of Art, Part III.

continuous συνεχής

contrary ἐναντίον Things are said to be contrary if they are the furthest apart or the most different within a genus or a species.

convinced, be πιστεύειν

conviction πίστις Syn: "strong belief."

country district δῆμος See "*deme*."

country χώρα

custom Syn: "usage."

customary εἰωθός

dactyl δάκτυλος A metrical foot in the form /xx or ˉ˘˘, that is, one syllable accented or long followed by two syllables unaccented or short, respectively.

definition ὅρος, ὁρισμός A *thought* or expression stating the nature or essence of a thing, i.e., "rational animal" for man.

delivery, art of ὑποκριτική

delivery, science of περὶ ὑποκριτικῆς

deme δῆμος A division or part of the countryside of a state, country district.

democracy πολιτεία One of the good forms of government.

demonstration ἀπόδειξις A proof through the cause.

design, by Same as "deliberately."

deus ex machina μηχανῇ An artificial device usually introduced by a bad poet to avoid a difficulty arising from a bad structure of a poem. Syn: "device."

diction λέξις The manner in which meaning is expressed.

differ διαφέρειν Be different; excel.

difference διαφορά Syn: "distinction" (sometimes). Usually, two different things fall under the same genus.

differentia διαφορά That which differentiates things coming under the same genus.

dignity σεμνότης

discriminate   Same as "judge."

dissimilar   ἀνόμοιος   Things are dissimilar if they differ in quality. Syn: "unlike."

distress   ὀδύνη

distress, extreme   Same as "agony."

dithyramb   διθύραμβος   In ancient Greece, a wild and emotional choral hymn in honor of Dionysus, the god of vegetation and wine.

doing   Same as *"acting."*

drama   δρᾶμα   A play, usually to be performed on stage.

dramatic   δραματικός   A dramatic poem, as opposed to a narrative poem, is a poem if it is presented (a) by performers, each representing a single agent in the play, or (b) by a narrator who speaks not in his own person but assumes in turn the role of the agents he represents.

elegiac   ἐλεγεῖος   Having the meter of an elegy, i.e., of a poem composed of hexameter couplets, the second line being called "a pentameter," i.e., a meter having only an accented syllable in the third and sixth feet.

elegy   ἐλεγεῖον   A poem (a) of lament and praise for the dead, or (b) written in a mournfully contemplative tone.

element   στοιχεῖον

emotion   πάθημα, πάθος   Syn: "feeling," "suffering," "passion."

end   τέλος   a thing aimed at, final cause, purpose; the result or outcome or last part.

end, accidental   A thing which is aimed at but is not proper to the kind of activity chosen, e.g., choosing surgery as a profession for the sake of making money.

end, final   A thing aimed at for its own sake, i.e., for the pleasure of it regardless of any consequences; e.g., listening to music, playing games, research for those who like this activity, etc. Syn: "end in itself," "end for its own sake."

end in itself   Same as "end, final."

end, proper   οἰκεῖον τέλος   For example, houses are the proper end of house-building, whether building houses is pleasant or not pleasant to the builder. Similarly, the proper end of an art is a work of that art, e.g., of housebuilding it is a house.

end, ultimate   For man, this is happiness; it is the most inclusive and most pleasant end, having as parts all other final ends taken in proportion to their contribution. Syn: "ultimate final end."

epic   ἔπος   A poem or poetry whose aim is the same as that of tragedy but which differs from a tragedy by being long and narrative and usually in hexameter, like the *Iliad* and the *Odyssey.* Syn: "heroic."

episode   ἐπεισόδιον   In a tragedy, the whole part which comes between two choral songs.

episodic poem   ἐπεισοδιῶδες ποίημα   A poem whose episodes do not follow from each other either of necessity or with probability.

equivocal   Same as "ambiguous."

error   ἁμάρτημα   That which results by an unintentional mistake in judgment.

error   ἁμαρτία   The making of an unintentional mistake in judgment that leads to a tragic *action.*

essence   οὐσία, ἴδιον   The essence of a thing is its nature without the accidents in it, i.e., that part of it which endures while the thing exists and without which the name proper to it does not have the same meaning when predicated of it. For example, the dead body of a man is not a man, for his soul has ceased to exist in that body.

ethical   ἠθικός   Pertaining to matters dealing with human conduct or *actions*, whether virtuous or vicious.

ethics   περὶ ἠθικῆς   The science of conduct or *action.*

event   πρᾶγμα   A composite which includes *actions* and other kinds of activities, whether human or associated with human *actions* in some way.

example   παράδειγμα

excel   διαφέρειν   Syn: "be superior to."

exception, without   Same as "without qualification."

exode   ἔξοδος   The whole part of a tragedy after which there is no choral song.

expected   Same as "probable."

expression   λόγος   A symbolic representation of thought, whether of a term or of a combination of terms.

fact   ὄν, πρᾶγμα

fallacy   παραλογισμός   False reasoning. Syn: "paralogism."

false   ψευδής   The contrary of "true."

fear φόβος Pain or mental disturbance arising from an image of an impending evil, whether painful or destructive (1382a21–22).

fearful φοβερός

feeling πάθος; πάθημα Syn: "emotion," "suffering," "passion."

final end Same as "end, final."

fine καλός

finest κάλλιστος (a) A finest tragedy is one which is produced in accord with all the truths of the art of tragedy; (b) a species of tragedy (a) which ends in tragedy for the protagonist.

flute αὐλός

foreign name γλῶττα A name is said to be foreign to a group if it is not standard to it but is standard to another group (1457b3–6). Names which are not standard but are used in different dialects are regarded as foreign.

form εἶδος The nature of a thing without its matter, if any; species; form; kind.

form, visible μορφή, σχῆμα

fortune Same as "luck."

fortune, bad ἀτυχία Bad luck. Syn: "ill fortune."

fortune, good εὐτυχία Good luck (197a25–27).

friendship φιλία

function ἔργον

general That which is either universal, i.e., necessary or always, or most of the time, or approximate.

generation γένεσις A change of a subject with respect to its essence (i.e., nature or form) or with respect to its attribute (i.e., its quantity or quality or place). If with respect to its essence, the generation is called "unqualified"; if with respect to an attribute, it is called "qualified."

genus γένος A universal thought or term divisible into species and predicable of each of its species and of the individuals under each species.

gift, natural εὐφυΐα A power, mental or physical, inherited at birth and easily developed if used.

God θεός For Aristotle, an immaterial and separate substance, also called "Prime Mover"; for the multitude, any of the anthropomorphic gods believed in by the common people or most of the ancient Greeks.

god   θεός   Any of the other immaterial substances acting as movers
    in the universe or of those believed to be gods.
good   ἀγαθός   The good of man is happiness; and if not happiness,
    any means or end in itself which contributes to happiness or to
    the excellence or perfection of a thing.
government   πολιτεία
grievous   οἰκτρός   Syn: "sorrowful."
habit   συνήθεια   See Commentaries, Section 1, Comm. 13.
habit   ἕξις   A stable disposition or quality of a thing in general,
    whether acquired or possessed in some other way.
happiness   εὐδαιμονία   The most pleasant and virtuous activity of man.
harmony   ἁρμονία   Harmony; intonation.
he   ὁ   (a) The pronoun is used for either sex, and similarly for "his"
    and "him"; (b) it is also used only for a male human being. This
    convention is limited to the translation and partly to the Com-
    mentaries and Theory of Art.
heroic   ἡρωικός   Pertaining to things dealing with or characteristic
    of great deeds or heroes or bravery or nobility or verse or epic
    poetry. Syn: "epic."
heroic meter   Usually the epic hexameter.
heroic poem   Same as "epic."
him, his   See "he."
history   ἱστορία   An account of particular events happening during
    a period or to an individual man or group of men but without
    any tendency to generalize those events.
honor   τιμή   A sign or an external good bestowed on someone of
    great worth (1123b17–21, 1361a27–30).
iamb   ἴαμβος   A metrical foot of two syllables, the first unaccented
    or short and the second accented or long, respectively.
iambic, adj.   ἰαμβικός   Pertaining to lines or meters or verse by the
    use of iambs; lampooning by the use of iambs. Sometimes
    "iambic" is used to mean an iambic poem.
ideal   παράδειγμα   Something assumed to be perfect with respect
    to some principle, e.g., a straight line. Syn: "model."
imitation   μίμησις   A copy or representation or idealization of an
    object which exists or existed or is thought to have existed; an
    act of copying or representing or idealizing that object.
impossible   ἀδύνατον   That which cannot exist as a thing or a fact.
in accord with   Same as "according to."

incongruous ὑπεναντίον

inconsistent ἀνώμαλος One whose *thoughts* and *actions* are often not in accord with his character.

inconsistent ὑπεναντίον Statements or *thoughts* which lead to contradiction.

indirectly κατὰ συμβεβηκός Syn: "accidentally."

indivisible ἀδιαίρετον That which cannot be divided in a certain manner, whether as a quantity or as a species into further species or according to some other principle.

inflection πτῶσις See lines 1457a18-23.

in general ὅλως

innate Same as "congenital."

inquiry μέθοδος Systematic inquiry.

insofar as ᾗ Syn: "*qua*," "to the extent that."

intention προαίρεσις A choice of the apparently best of the alternatives deliberated upon, but the apparently best need not be good but only appear to be so (1113a2–7).

intonation ἁρμονία

in virtue of Same as "according to."

involvement πλοκή

joint ἄρθρον

judge, v. κρίνειν Syn: "discriminate."

judgment γνώμη Right judgment by a fair-minded man as such concerning particulars, sometimes even universals (1143a19–35).

justice δικαιοσύνη

kingship βασιλεία A form of government ruled by one man who excels in virtue by far all other citizens.

kinship φιλία

knowledge γνῶσις It is a genus having as species "sensation," "opinion," "scientific knowledge," etc.

lamentation θρῆνος; κομμός

lampoon, v. ἰαμβίζειν

letter στοιχεῖον An element of a word.

life ζωή; βίος (sometimes).

life, way of βίος The manner in which one lives.

like ὅμοιος Usually, the same in quality. Syn: "similar."

likely εἰκός Syn: "probable," "expected."

likeness εἰκών For example, a picture or a painting is a likeness of what it represents or portrays.

luck   τύχη   An accidental mover. Luck or what results from luck be-
    longs to one who can or might deliberate or act, i.e., to man.
    "Chance" is the genus of "luck." 195b31–198a13. Syn: "fortune."
luck, bad   ἀτυχία
luck, good   εὐτυχία
ludicrous   γελεῖος   Causing laughter. Syn: "ridiculous."
lyre   κιθάρα   In ancient Greece, the instrument was triangular in
    shape and had seven strings.
magnanimity   μεγαλοψυχία   Greatness of soul (1123a34–5a35).
make, v.   Same as "produce."
man   ἄνθρωπος   A human being, male or female. Syn. "person."
man   ἀνήρ   A male human being, especially an adult.
manly   Same as "brave."
mathematical probability   See "probability, mathematical."
may   Same as "can," "possible."
mean, v.   Same as "signify."
mean, n.   μέσον   That which lies between two opposite extremes,
    e.g., a virtue.
metaphor   μεταφορά   (a) A name which replaces in an expression an-
    other name, whether it is related to the name replaced as a
    genus of it, or as a species of it, or as a species to another species
    under the same genus, or as a name analogous to it. (b) The
    whole expression after the replacement as in (a) (1457b6–9).
meter   μέτρον   Meter, as in verse.
metrical art   μετρική
metrics, art of   Same as "metrical art."
metrics, science of   περὶ μετρικῆς
middle   μέσον
mime   μῖμος   An ancient Greek farce or exaggerated comedy in-
    tended to mimic or ridicule people or events.
misfortune   δυστυχία   Bad luck of great magnitude.
mistake   ἁμαρτία; ἁμάρτημα
mob rule   Same as "people's rule."
model   Same as "ideal."
moral   Same as "ethical."
motion   κίνησις   A change with respect to quantity or quality or
    place. Syn: "movement."
movement   Same as "motion."
mute   ἄφωνον   A consonant letter (1456b25–31).

name   ὄνομα   (a) A noun. (b) A noun or a verb or an inflection, thus the word "name" being the genus of these three.

narrative   διήγησις   An account of events, whether real or poetic, usually given by one man.

natural   Same as "physical."

natural gift   εὐφυία   An unusual physical or mental power inherited at birth, such as mathematical or musical ability for research or composing or athletic ability.

nature   φύσις   The form of a physical substance, as discussed in Part III of Aristotle's Theory of Art.

necessary   ἀναγκαῖον   That which must be always.

noble   καλός   Being of great worth or value and deserving honor. For example, Clara Barton and the fathers of our Constitution were noble Americans.

nome   νόμος   A solo poem accompanied by the lyre.

noun   ὄνομα   A composite vocal sound which has meaning that includes no time, and no part of which as a part has meaning; used as a genus, it includes also verbs, inflections, cases, etc.

number   ἀριθμός   A whole number, called "a natural number" by mathematicians, except the number 1.

object, n.   That which exists, or may exist, or cannot exist, e.g., the Woolworth building, or a building twice as high, or a square with unequal diagonals, respectively.

oligarchy   ὀλιγαρχία   A government by the few, usually the rich or the powerful.

opinion   δόξα   A belief of that which is possible and may or may not exist.

ornament   κόσμος   An ornamental name. See Commentaries, Section 21, Comm. 10.

parode   πάροδος   In a tragedy, the first spoken part, taken as a whole, of the chorus.

parody   παρῳδία   A poem ridiculing a writer or his work by imitating the style but distorting or changing the content nonsensically or absurdly or incongruously.

part   μέρος, μόριον

people, common   See, "common people."

people's rule   δημοκρατία   A state ruled by the common people or lower classes, usually led by a demagogue. Syn: "popular rule," "ochlocracy," "mob rule."

perceive   Same as "sense," v.

performance   ἔργον; ἀγών   A play in action.

performer   ὑποκριτής   An actor who represents a character or agent in a play.

persuasive   πιθανός   One who can persuade others by making himself credible or by using reasoning or by arousing the emotions of others; a thing which can so persuade, e.g., a speech. Syn: "plausible."

philosophy   φιλοσοφία   The science of the highest and most important principles of things. Syn: "wisdom."

physical   φυσικός   Related in some way to what has a nature.

pitiful   ἐλεεινός   Deserving to be pitied and causing others to pity him because of undeserved misfortune.

pity   ἔλεος   Pain in a man caused by what appears to be a destructive or painful evil which befalls another who does not deserve it and of which the man would think that he himself or someone close to him might be the victim in the near future (1385b13–16).

play   Same as "drama."

pleasure   ἡδονή

plot   μῦθος   The composition of events represented in a play.

poem   ποίημα   An imitation having a plot with parts, being a whole with a beginning and a middle and an end, each of its parts of which gives pleasure according to its appropriate nature.

poetic art   ποιητική   The art of producing good poems.

poetics   περὶ ποιητικῆς   The science concerned with the truths which must be used to produce a good poem. Syn: "science of poetic art." It is defined in Part V of Aristotle's Theory of Art.

poetry   ποιήματα   poems collectively.

poetry, the making of   The production of poems.

politics   πολιτική   (a) The science of government; (b) the art of governing well.

political science   περὶ πολιτικῆς

possible   δυνατόν   That which can exist.

power   δύναμις   That which can produce or act or theorize.

practical   πρακτικός   Pertaining to *action*. For example, a practical science is a science of *actions*, which are activities as ends in themselves.

Prime Mover   Same as "God."

principle   ἀρχή   A beginning or starting point, e.g., the principles of a science, or a person who started a fight, or the ultimate parts of a thing, or the end or purpose of a thing.

probable εἰκός That which occurs most of the time or is usually expected. Syn: "expected," "likely."

probability, mathematical The relative frequency of an event; it ranges from 0 to 1.

produce ποιεῖν Same as "make."

product ποίημα Something made, usually by art.

production ποίησις The making of something by using certain materials. Production differs from theorizing, which is investigating principles and demonstrating from them; and it differs from *action*, which need not use any materials. Syn: "making."

prologue πρόλογος The whole part of a tragedy which precedes the entrance of the chorus.

proper ἴδιον Syn: "special," "property," "essence" (sometimes).

property ἴδιον Usually that which, not being the essence of a thing, belongs to it and to no other thing. Of animals, for example, writing is a property of man alone.

prose λόγος ψιλός, λόγος

proportion ἀναλογία Syn: "analogy."

prudence φρόνησις A disposition in man by which he can deliberate truly concerning his conduct for the sake of a good life (1140a24–b30).

purification (of emotions) Same as "catharsis."

purpose ἔργον Syn: "function."

qua ᾗ Same as "insofar as it is."

qualification, without See "without qualification."

quality ποιόν, ποιότης

quantity ποσόν, ποσότης

reason λόγος An expression signifying a composite thought, e.g., "four is a number," and the definition "rational animal"; a composite thought. See Aristotle's Theory of Art, Part II.

reason Same as "cause."

reasoning, false Same as "fallacy."

recognition ἀναγνώρισις See lines 1451a29–b8.

refutation ἔλεγχος Rejection of a thesis or hypothesis or statement by logic or evidence.

repugnant μιαρόν

reputation δόξα

resolution λύσις The part of the plot which immediately follows
the change from good fortune to bad fortune until the end of
the tragedy (1455b28–31).

reversal περιπέτεια A change of events in accord with necessity
or probability to the contrary of what is expected (1452a22–9).

rhetoric ῥητορική The art of persuading others.

rhetoric, science of περὶ ῥητορικῆς The science which investigates
the means of persuading others.

science ἐπιστήμη Systematic knowledge of the principles of a subject
along with the demonstration of theorems from those principles.

scientific knowledge ἐπιστήμη Knowledge in a science of things
through their causes.

sensation αἴσθησις Syn: "perception."

sense, n. αἴσθησις Syn: "The power of sensing."

serious σπουδαῖος Of some importance.

shrewd δεινός Able to act successfully by using any means to
achieve a practical end, whether good or bad (1144a23–6).

signify σημαίνειν Syn: "mean." For example, the word "circle"
signifies or means or stands for a circle.

similar Same as "like."

skill ἕξις ποιητική Ability, usually acquired, to produce primarily
a work of art.

solution Syn: resolution.

song μέλος

sophist σοφιστής A man who pretends or appears to be wise but is
not wise.

sorrowful Same as "grievous."

soul ψυχή In a man, the soul is his form, which amounts to his powers of nutrition, sensation, thinking, motion, etc.

soul, greatness of Same as "magnanimity," 1123a34–5a35.

species εἶδος The kinds into which a genus is divided. As a universal, it exists in the mind of man, or else as a symbol, whether
vocal or written or in some other form.

spectacle ὄψις

spectator θεατής

spectators θεαταί, θέατρον Syn: "audience."

speech λόγος Vocal language.

stade στάδιον One-eighth mile long.

stage σκηνή

standard κύριον A name used ordinarily by a group (1457b1–6).

stasimon στάσιμον A choral song without anapests or trochees (1452b23–24).

state πόλις A small nation or country usually with a population hardly exceeding 100,000 citizens.

story λόγος

strange ξενικόν A name which is not standard, e.g., a foreign name or a metaphor or any of the others (1457b1–3, 1458a22–23).

substance οὐσία

suburb περιοικίς

succeed κατορθοῦν To achieve a good which one is aiming at.

suffer πάσχειν

suffering πάθος; πάθημα

syllable συλλαβή (1456b20–25).

task ἔργον

terrible δεινός

theater θέατρον

theorem θεώρημα A conclusion demonstrated from premises through the cause.

think, v. νοεῖν A mental activity contrasted with sensing, feeling, etc.

think, v. διανοεῖν To combine concepts, as in "five is odd."

through Same as "because."

tragedy τραγῳδία Defined in lines 1449b24–8.

translation μετάφρασις (a) The process of translating; (b) the language into which something has been translated.

trial and error πεῖρα

trochee τροχαῖος In language, a metrical foot of the form ˉ˘, or /x, that is, consisting of a long or accented syllable followed by a short or unaccented syllable, respectively, as in "Pe-ter."

Troy, ancient Ἴλιον

truth ἀλήθεια A *thought* or statement which signifies a fact.

ugly αἰσχρός

ultimate end See "end, ultimate."

universal καθόλου A thought or expression predicable of or applicable to an indefinite number of things.

universally καθόλου

unlike Same as "dissimilar."

unpersuasive ἀπίθανος

unreasonable ἄλογον Contrary to reason or beliefs or expectation.

usage   ἔθος   Syn: "custom."

useful   χρήσιμος   A means to an end, e.g., as in "food is useful for life."

verb   ῥῆμα   A name which includes also time; e.g., "he runs," "they ran," etc.

verse   ἔμμετρον, μέτρον   (sometimes). A poem or any other work in language with meter.

verse without harmony   ψιλομετρία

vice   κακία   The contrary of "virtue."

virtue   ἀρετή   Usually an acquired habit disposing a man to right *action* or pursuit of truth or both, which are necessary to happiness.

virtuous   σπουδαῖος

voice   φωνή

vulgar   φορτικός, φαῦλος   (sometimes).

whole   ὅλον   That of which no part is missing (1450b26–31).

wisdom   σοφία   Knowledge of the most noble things.

wish   βούλησις   Desire of the good or the apparent good.

without exception   ἁπλῶς

without qualification   Same as "without exception."

with respect to   Same as "according to."

woman   γυνή

wonder, n.   θαῦμα

GREEK-ENGLISH

ἀγαθόν   good
ἀγών   competition; performance
ἀδιαίρετον   indivisible
ἀδύνατον   impossible
αἴσθησις   sense, n., power of sensation
αἴσθησις   sensation, perception
αἰτία, αἴτιον   cause, *reason*
ἀκριβής   accurate
ἀλήθεια, ἀληθές   truth
ἄλογον   unreasonable
ἁμάρτημα   error; mistake
ἁμαρτία   error; mistake
ἀμφιβολία   ambiguity, equivocation
ἀναγκαῖον   necessary
ἀναγνώρισις   recognition
ἀναλογία   analogy, proportion
ἀνάπαιστος   anapest
ἀνδρεῖος   brave, manly
ἀνήρ   *man* (male only)
ἄνθρωπος   man (male or female)
ἀνόμοιος   unlike, dissimilar
ἀνώμαλος   inconsistent [of man's *actions* and *thoughts*]
ἀπίθανος   unpersuasive
ἁπλοῦς   simple
ἁπλῶς   without qualification, without exception
ἀρετή   virtue
ἄρθρον   joint
ἀριθμός   whole number, except 1.
ἀριστοκρατία   aristocracy
ἁρμονία   harmony; intonation
ἀρχή   beginning, principle
ἄρχων   archon
ἄστυ   city
ἄτοπον   absurd
ἀτυχία   bad luck, bad fortune
αὐλός   flute
αὐτόματον   chance; *chance*
ἄφωνον   mute
βαρβαρισμός   barbarism, jargon, solecism

βασιλεία   kingship
βίος   life; way of life
βούλησις   wish
γελοῖος   ludicrous, ridiculous
γένεσις   generation
γένος   kind; genus; family
γλῶττα   foreign name
γνώμη   *judgment*
γνῶσις   knowledge
γυνή   woman
δάκτυλος   dactyl
δεινός   terrible; shrewd
δέσις   complication
δημοκρατία   people's rule, mob rule
δῆμος   *deme*, country district
διά   because, through, by, by means of
διανοεῖν   *think*
διαφέρειν   differ; excel
διαφορά   difference; differentia
διήγησις   narrative
διθύραμβος   dithyramb
δικαιοσύνη   justice
διότι   because, through, by, by means of
δόξα   opinion; reputation
δρᾶμα   drama, play
δραματικός   dramatic
δύναμις   ability, power, capability
δύναται   can, may, is possible
δυνατόν   possible
δυστυχία   misfortune
ἔθος   usage, custom
εἶδος   species; form; kind
εἰκός   probable, expected, likely
εἰκών   portrait, likeness
εἰωθός   customary
ἐλεγεῖον   elegy
ἐλεγεῖος   elegiac
ἔλεγχος   refutation
ἐλεεινός   pitiful

ἔλεος pity
ἔμμετρος verse, with meter
ἐναντίον contrary
ἐνέργεια activity
ἕξις habit
ἕξις, ποιητική skill
ἔξοδος exode
ἐπεισόδιον episode
ἐπεισοδιώδης episodic
ἐπιστήμη science; scientific knowledge of a fact
ἔπος epic; epic poem
ἔργον task; purpose, function; performance
εὐδαιμονία happiness
εὐτυχία good fortune, good luck
εὐφυής gifted by nature
ζῷον animal (including man)
ᾗ *qua*, insofar as, to the extent that
ἡδονή pleasure
ἠθικῆς, περὶ science of ethics, ethics
ἠθικός ethical, moral
ἦθος character of a man
ἡρωικός heroic; epic
θαῦμα wonder
θεός god; Prime Mover, God
θεώρημα theorem
θεωρητικός theoretical
θηρίον brute, animal (except man)
θρῆνος lamentation
ἰαμβεῖον iambic verse
ἰαμβίζειν lampoon, v.
ἰαμβικός iambic
ἴαμβος iamb
ἴδιον proper, special; property; essence (sometimes)
Ἴλιον ancient Troy
ἱστορία history (of particulars)
κάθαρσις catharsis, purification
καθόλου universal; universally
κακία vice, evil
κακός bad, vicious

κάλλιστος finest
καλός noble; beautiful; fine
κατά according to
κατορθοῦν *succeed*
κιθάρα lyre
κίνησις motion, movement
κοινός common
κομμός *commos*, lamentation
κράτιστος best
κρείττων better, superior to
κρίνειν judge, discriminate
κύριον standard
κωμῳδία comedy
λέξις diction
λόγος speech; reason; prose; expression; dialogue; treatise;
  story; argument
λόγος, ψιλός prose
λύσις resolution; solution
μεγαλοψυχία magnanimity
μέθοδος *inquiry*, systematic inquiry
μέλος song
μέρος part
μεταβολή change
μεταφορά metaphor
μέσον middle; mean
μετρική metrics, art of
μετρικῆς, περὶ science of metrics
μέτρον meter, verse
μηχανῆ device, *deus ex machina*
μιαρόν repugnant
μίμημα imitation
μίμησις imitation
μῖμος mime
μόριον part
μῦθος plot
νοεῖν think, v.
νόμος nome; custom; law
ξενικόν strange
ὀδύνη distress

οἰκτρός   grievous, sorrowful
ὀλιγαρχία   oligarchy
ὅλον   whole
ὅλως   in general
ὁμαλός   consistent
ὅμοιος   similar, like
ὄν   thing, fact, being
ὄνομα   noun; name
ὀργή   anger
ὁρισμός   definition
ὅρος   definition
οὐσία   essence, substance
ὄψις   spectacle
πάθημα   emotion, feeling, passion, suffering
πάθος   passion, feeling, suffering, emotion
παράδειγμα   example; model, ideal
παραλογισμός   false reasoning, fallacy
πάροδος   parode
παρῳδία   parody
πάσχειν   suffer
πεῖρα   trial and error
περιωδυνία   agony, extreme distress
περιοικίς   suburb
περιπέτεια   reversal
πιθανός   persuasive; plausible
πιστεύειν   convinced, be
πίστις   conviction, strong belief
πλοκή   involvement
ποιεῖν   produce, make; act
ποίημα   poem; something produced, product
ποιήματα   poetry
ποίησις   action; production, making; production of poems
ποιητής   poet; maker, producer
ποιητική   art of poetry, poetic art
ποιητικῆς, περὶ   poetics, science of poetic art
ποιόν, ποιότης   quality
πόλις   state
πολιτεία   democracy; government
πολιτική   art of politics; politics

πολιτικῆς, περὶ science of politics
πονηρός bad, base (adj.)
ποσόν, ποσότης quantity
πρᾶγμα event, thing; fact
πρακτικός practical
πρᾶξις *action*, doing
πράττων agent, character in a play
προαίρεσις intention
πρόλογος prologue
προσῳδία pronunciation
πτῶσις inflection
ῥῆμα verb
σεμνότης dignity
σημαίνειν signify, mean
σκηνή stage
σοφιστής sophist
σοφία wisdom
σπουδαῖος virtuous; serious
στάδιον stade
στάσιμον stasimon
στοιχεῖον element; a letter of a word
συλλαβή syllable
συμβεβηκός accident
συμβεβηκός, κατὰ accidentally, indirectly
σύμφυτος innate, congenital
σύνδεσμος connective
συνεχής continuous
συνήθεια habit
σῶμα body
τέλειος complete
τέλος end
τέχνη art
τιμή honor
τόπος place
τραγῳδία tragedy
τροχαῖος trochee
τύχη luck, fortune
ὑπεναντίον inconsistent; incongruous
ὑποκριτής performer

ὑπόληψις belief
φαίνεσθαι appear
φαῦλος bad; vulgar
φαυλότερος inferior
φιλανθρωπία compassion
φιλία friendship; kinship
φιλοσοφία philosophy
φοβερός fearful
φόβος fear
φορτικός vulgar
φρόνησις prudence
φύσει by nature
φύσις nature
φωνή voice, vocal sound
χορικόν choral
χορός chorus
χρήσιμος useful
χρηστός cogent
χώρα country
ψευδής false
ψιλομετρία verse without harmony
ψιλὸς λόγος prose
ψυχή soul

INDEX

history, of particulars, 11
Homer, 2, 3, 4, 10, 35
  how he uses fallacies, 31
  imitates Achilles as better, 18
  Odysseus on Ithaca shores, 32
  praised by Aristotle, 29, 30
  use of metaphor, 31

I

iambic, 4
Icadius, 35
Icarius, 35
Iliad, 4, 29, 37
  as one, 24
  has epic structure, 21
  lines in, 37
  use of *deus ex machina*, 15
imitation, artistic, def., 118
  artistic, discussed, 117–8
  differentiae, 1, 3
  manner of, 3
  of objects as qualified, 33
  of one *action*, 10
  of three kinds, 32
  should excel what is actual, 17
inflection, def., 24
Iphigenia in Tauris, 18, 19
  best disposition with recognition, 16
  outline of, 20
  recognition in, 13
Iphigenia, inconsistent in *Iphigenia in Aulis*, 17
  recognition of, 18
Ixion, 21

J

joint, def., 23

L

language, as means, 1
lengthened name, def., 26
letter, def., 23
likeness, 1, 2
Little Iliad, 29
lucid diction, 26
ludicrous, def., 5
Lynceus, 12, 19
lyre, 1, 2

M

Magnes, 3
magnitude, important in tragedy, 9

limits in tragedy, 9
making, same as "production"
Margites, 4
masculine name, def., 26
Medea, 16
Medea, use of *deus ex machina*, 17
Megarians, 3
Melanippe, unfit character, 17
Menelaus, base in *Orestes*, unnecessary, 17
Menelaus, in the *Orestes*, 36
Merope, 16
metaphor, appropriate to iambic poems, 28
  belongs to the gifted, 28
  def., 25
  most important, 28
meter, 1
  as part of rhythm, 4
Methodics, 96
middle, in tragedy, def., 9
mime, 1
mistakes, kinds in poems, 32
  none should be made, 33
Mitys, statue of, 12
Mnasitheus, 37
Mynniscus, 36
Mysians, 31

N

name, altered, def., 26
  double, def., 24
  feminine, def., 26
  foreign, def., 25
  kinds, 25
  lengthened, def., 26
  masculine, def., 26
  newly-coined, def., 25
  shortened, def., 26
  simple, def., 24
  standard, def., 25
nature, according to, 1
nature, as the form of a thing, 18
Nicochares, 2
Niobe, 21
nome, 2
noun, def., 24

O

objections, answers to, 32–36
Odysseus, 18, 35
  on Ithaca shores, 32